Praise for *Parent Like It Matters*

"I keep a copy of the book by my [...] reminder that I am working to buil[...] my own daughter and to ensure sh[...] fident, knowing woman."

—*The Washington Post*

"To matter is a universal human need, and both parent and child benefit from the process and the outcome of raising girls who are critical thinkers and change-makers. . . . This recommended title has insights and practical tips for raising change-making girls."

—*Library Journal* (starred review)

"Johnson Dias's forthright advice successfully calls upon parents to join their girls in creating the changes they wish to see. Her wide-ranging guidance shouldn't be missed."

—*Publishers Weekly*

"A powerful resource for caregivers trying to raise courageous girls, this book is an eloquent testimony from a caring mother and a practical parenting guide from an acclaimed sociologist. It's my go-to and my how-to. And if you need advice on everything from introducing your tween to social media to helping her lift her voice for change in this world, it should be yours too."

—KWAME ALEXANDER, *New York Times* bestselling author of *Light for the World to See*

"*Parent Like It Matters* gives me hope for girls to dream themselves into the future as healed, whole, powerful, actualized women, because this book will help to create healed, whole, powerful, actualized parents to support them on their journey."

—EBONYJANICE MOORE, hip-hop womanist scholar and founder of Black Girl Mixtape and The Free People Project

"*Parent Like It Matters* is a stunning and pathbreaking how-to guide and memoir for every mom, dad, or caregiver who believes in rearing children to be healthy individuals and caring citizens. Combining her talents as a leading sociologist with the wisdom of her grandmother and the experience of raising talented change agents in her community, Dr. Johnson Dias makes clear in this beautifully written book that there may be no more important responsibility."

—KHALIL GIBRAN MUHAMMAD, author of
The Condemnation of Blackness

"If you have a Black girl in your life—daughter, niece, neighbor, student—you owe it to her to read this book. Part memoir, part advice column, part workbook, *Parent Like it Matters* is a wholly original, deeply challenging, and expansively joyful guide to walking beside the girl in your life as she finds voice, courage, purpose, and self. I am in awe of the deeply introspective and profoundly honest mother, scholar, and change-maker that is Janice Johnson Dias."

—MELISSA HARRIS-PERRY, Maya Angelou Presidential Chair at
Wake Forest University

"I am beyond proud of my mom and *Parent Like It Matters*! This book is a combination of faith in the power of children's voices and a guide for focus-driven parenting that will inspire a new generation of young change-makers."

—MARLEY DIAS, author of *Marley Dias Gets It Done*

"In *Parent Like It Matters*, Dr. Janice Johnson Dias offers an impressive and bold road map for those who seek to engage passion and joy as essential elements of developing girls who thrive. Her honest and rigorous offering is a gift to parents, educators, and all adults in search of tools to cultivate the brilliance of our girls."

—MONIQUE W. MORRIS, author of *Pushout* and founder of the
National Black Women's Justice Institute

Parent Like It Matters

Parent Like It Matters

How to Raise Joyful, Change-Making Girls

Janice Johnson Dias, PhD

BALLANTINE BOOKS

NEW YORK

2022 Ballantine Books Trade Paperback Edition

Published in the United States by Ballantine Books, an imprint of Random House, a division of Penguin Random House LLC, New York.

BALLANTINE and the HOUSE colophon are registered trademarks of Penguin Random House LLC.

Originally published in hardcover in the United States by Ballantine Books, an imprint of Random House, a division of Penguin Random House LLC, in 2020.

Library of Congress Cataloging-in-Publication Data

Names: Dias, Janice Johnson, author.
Title: Parent like it matters: how to raise joyful, change-making girls / Janice Johnson Dias, PhD.
Description: New York: Ballantine Group, 2021. | Includes bibliographical references.
Identifiers: LCCN 2020029217 (print) | LCCN 2020029218 (ebook) | ISBN 9781984819642 | ISBN 9781984819635 (ebook)
Subjects: LCSH: Parenting. | Girls—Psychology. | Parent and child—Psychological aspects.
Classification: LCC HQ755.8 .D48953 2021 (print) | LCC HQ755.8 (ebook) | DDC 306.874—dc23
LC record available at lccn.loc.gov/2020029217
LC ebook record available at lccn.loc.gov/2020029218

randomhousebooks.com

1st Printing

Book design by Diane Hobbing

To Marley, thank you for teaching me the truest meaning of love.

To Scotty, thank you for being by my side on this journey.

To parents, thanks for teaching me that parenting is a full contact sport.

Foreword

Jacqueline Woodson

In early 2002 I gave birth to my first child—a girl born weighing just six pounds. It had been a long birth and a stressful labor, the baby finally pushing through only after the doctors had begun looking for an operating room in which they could perform a C-section. I was thirty-nine and had spent the previous six years planning for the day when I would be called Mommy. I knew I wanted a child. I knew the gender did not matter. I knew I was at a point in my life when I could devote time to being a mother. I was not caught up in some kind of dream birth plan, so a C-section wasn't stressing me at all. According to the doctors, the baby was two weeks late and her heart rate was spiking. I wanted her safe. I wanted her alive. I wanted her out of me. And, as she would do for the next eighteen years, just when we thought we'd have to make a new plan for getting her to show up, she showed up—a crop of black curls crowning. And ten minutes later, I was suddenly a mother.

Looking back on that time, when I spent long hours moving through the pages of *What to Expect When You're Expecting,* I realize the book I wish I had had at my bedside was *Parent Like It Matters.* Instead of Dr. Spock, I wish I had had Dr. Johnson Dias. Her soothing cadence only enhances the brilliance on the pages you're about to read. What Janice Johnson Dias brings to us here is a manifesto for raising loving, intentional, brilliant, change-making young people. And while those of us raising girls will find this book astonishingly beneficial, there is something here for all of us. As evidenced by her own daughter, Marley Dias, a young internationally known activist, author, and scholar, *Parent Like It Matters* is a present-day blueprint for shining a light on ourselves and our daughters so that they can grow into the amazing young people we hoped to bring them here to be.

Like so many parents, my partner and I concerned ourselves with the education of our child—which schools would be the best fit and how we would access them. Too late we learned that our neighborhood had changed so rapidly that our zoned school had seemingly overnight become more than 90 percent white. We had both been taught, through our own upbringings, the importance of education. Both of us eschewed private education for public. When our daughter was born, we remained intentional about circling her with extended family, both chosen and biological. We believed in the Village of Child Raising, the importance of our daughter knowing there are many ways to have family. And because, for a long time, I had not known my own father, we were intentional about our daughter spending time with her dad, a close friend of ours who lived in California.

Five months after our daughter's birth, her father and his wife gave birth to a girl. This shifted our intentions once again. We wanted to make sure the sisters grew up close, making a point to come together for every birthday and holiday. Six years later, my partner gave birth to our son. And again, our family and our intentions shifted with the hopes not only of ensuring that our young people had room to figure out who they were and all that they could become, but also of blanketing them with the love of their extended family.

And yet . . .

We hadn't truly thought about what kind of impact we wanted our children to have on the world. We hadn't thought about intentionally working toward their happiness, health, well-being. We had figured because we were activists, our children would naturally grow up to be activists. Because we were hardworking, our kids would be so too. And what about self-confidence? Didn't this too just naturally flow from mothers to daughters?

Well . . . I've come to learn it does not. As my daughter grew, I began to see how she saw herself reflected through the gaze of the world around her. A world that too often didn't see her beauty. Her brilliance. Her shine. I knew then that other tools were needed. Even with our wonderful village, our nightly conversations around the dinner table, our showing up for every school play and parent-teacher conference. Even through the years of piano lessons and dance classes and huge birthday parties. Even as we traveled abroad for months at a time each year to help our kids understand more of the world and worked to expand their dietary and social palates. Even as we refused to shy away from conversations about alcohol, sex, toxic friendships. Even as we thought we were parenting intentionally, there was still so much we didn't know.

From volunteerism to visualization to living with purpose. From igniting social action to change-making. From the love we feel the first time we hold our daughters in our arms to the eternity of love that comes after that, our parenting truly matters. Janice's warm and conversational tone brings us comfort and confidence, and her well-conceived "assignments" put us to task and show us the work we've yet to do. By the end of this book, we are able to see ourselves as parents through a new lens. And finally, we can truly see our children in all of their wonder and possibility. I've learned that it's never too late to begin to parent like it matters—with love, with intention, with gratitude.

As parents we often talk about how fast our children grow—the long nights and short years. Here's to all of us using those years wisely, to create a better world and to teach our children to do the same.

Welcome to *Parent Like It Matters*. Both you and your child will be better because of this book. I wish you peace, joy, and so much love on the journey.

Contents

Introduction

Dr. Ruth Simmons was the first Black president of an Ivy League university. She was also the youngest of twelve children born to a sharecropping family in East Texas. Growing up, she was expected to become a domestic worker. But Dr. Simmons dreamed of more. Enthralled by learning, she asked her mother if she might one day go to college. The look on her mother's face told her more clearly than any words could that it was an impossible idea. And yet not only did Dr. Simmons attend college, in 2000 she became president of Brown University. Her very presence in that office signaled to young women that they didn't have to put limits on their dreams.

What made the difference for Dr. Simmons? "I knew somewhere that this world I lived in, a world of segregation and bigotry, wasn't really the real world," she explained. "And what I had to do was go outside it—and that's what everybody has to do. They have to find a way to be a part of that larger world."

Her words offer a stunning insight into one of the core truths we must teach our girls—our potential transcends our immediate circumstances. For parents, raising girls who can dream as big as Ruth Simmons did is a matter of intentionality. We must coach our daughters that if they can dream it, they can create it for themselves and their community. But first they must learn how to tap the resources that will help them manifest their vision in the larger world.

In order for this to happen, we, as parents, must be their chief resource and their conduit to this transformation and action.

Parent Like It Matters examines how parents and caregivers can help girls understand, find, and operate from this perspective: The liberty we seek for ourselves is possible for all. The book explores how we can instill an adventurous, can-do spirit in girls while making sure they also feel safe—safe to move about, safe to make mistakes, safe to speak their minds, safe to invent worlds. It discusses the importance of grounding girls in family and cultural history, as well as negotiations surrounding personal appearance, scheduling, academics, extracurricular activities, friendships, and social pressure. My goal is to provide caregivers with a strong yet pliable framework within which girls can understand and appreciate themselves, so that the ground beneath their feet will always feel sure.

Informed by personal experiences, supported by expert insights, and illuminated by anecdotes from my decade of working with girls, this book offers a blueprint to embolden our girls to be critical thinkers, fearless doers, and joyful change agents for our future. It consciously and deliberately guides girls and parents to grasp their critical role in transforming our world, starting with themselves and their communities. The fact is, left to chance, self-realization and a change-making mindset become something of a crapshoot. Our girls might still manage it, as Ruth Simmons did, especially if they have teachers or mentors who will stand in the gap for them. But what if they don't?

Parent Like It Matters is all about *making sure.*

I, like you, know that parenting is challenging. Regardless of what fun we had making our children, by the time they arrive in the world they have already made several demands of us. We have had to change our diet, adjust our schedules, reconfigure our homes, develop new ways of living—and these efforts are only the beginning. Over the course of their lives they will demand more, and we must be ready to respond as best we can, knowing that we will succeed and fail along the way. But when we parent like it matters, the successes and the failures will enrich us. Parenting like it matters will give our lives deeper meaning and enhance our sense of joyfulness.

To matter is a universal human need, and when you parent like it matters you are engaged in a reciprocal relationship with your children, both of you benefiting from the process and the outcome. This undertaking will make it clear that your parental choices are deeply influential and inspirational. People want and need to be inspired. When people are inspired, they are lifted above their circumstances and are more hopeful. If you can be the one who inspires your children, by encouragement and through modeling, you will also have demonstrated that you matter! But choosing to matter is a daily choice. You will have to give yourself options every day in the way you live and parent. In this book I have offered some ways for you to do this. Choose the ways that work best for you. But know that you must first matter to yourself so that you can model for your girl the ways in which she matters.

Parent Like It Matters explores how parents, caregivers, and community mentors can help girls create the lives they dream of, ones that are joyful and harmonious. To achieve these ends, the book also explains why we must teach girls to lift as they climb — and pull others along with them.

As parents or caregivers, our first task is to lay down the burdens of our past to make space for joy in raising our girls. Only then can we avoid feeling overwhelmed by the enormous work of creating a more just world, and only then can we move beyond paralyzing inaction toward strategic hopefulness. Furthermore, I offer a toolkit of how to help our girls cut through society's incessant chatter about who they *can* be, to determine for themselves who they *will* be.

What you'll find in this book is my life's work, which started in the classroom — as a student, as a professor myself, and then as an academic scholar, leading studies on public health and social stratification and inequality. Eventually it was the work in my own home, as co-parent to my daughter, Marley, and finally as founder and teacher at the GrassROOTS Community Foundation Super-Camp for girls.

From its inception, giving back was always a part of SuperCamp. In the first year, this group of five-year-olds read to the babies at a local daycare. It was important to me that girls see that regardless of their age they could always be of service to others. Those who were not great readers could draw with the babies. The practice of going weekly to the kindergarten unleashed in me the idea that if children grew up knowing and feeling that community service mattered, then they would and could help make the world a better and more harmonious place.

Over the next several years, I set out on a mission to train girls and their families to become healthy and to use their healthy energy to make a difference in the world. This commitment to public health and social justice became the foundation of my work.

I continued to lead the camp the following year, and I have led it now for ten summers. The camp moved from being a girls' camp to a family-centered camp. Though the girls receive most of the direct programming, the caregivers are partners in the work. The caregivers too have to perform with the girls in the final showcase, and they must participate in weekly community circle. Parents and their caregiving circle have to sign a contract to work collaboratively with us, and they must develop a shared plan of action for the girls. We maintain a listserve and WhatsApp group where we share information on health and issues affecting our community.

The journey of leading this camp and doing this work has taught me that caregivers want the best for their children, but we all struggle with modeling for our kids what the best looks like. I have also learned that girls trust their parents more than they trust others, and as such they will mimic and follow the actions of their parents, sometimes consciously, oftentimes unconsciously—even if it stymies or harms their development.

It is the experience of watching and learning how—and in what ways—parents matter for girls' well-being that prompted me to write this book. Girls and the parents I have trained and worked with have shown me that if we want things to change for the future, we have to start with right now, and we must start not only with children but with ourselves. More specifically, we must support those who care for children, namely their parents and their care circle. Children can only thrive when their parents and those who care for them also thrive.

SuperCamp helped me come to this understanding. The stories you will find here come from a decade of working with families. The majority of the characters are composites of girls and their families. With their permission, I have also profiled a few folks. Enjoy.

I started SuperCamp with five girls who were five years old; over time this work grew and I developed a framework to organize the work. I used the model of a tree to frame the programming because trees symbolize life and growth and I wanted to connect the girls' cultivation to the growth process that exists in nature. We call our youngest girls SEEDLINGS, because to me preadolescent youth are like seeds; they grow best when their basic needs are met. The Seedlings program therefore emphasizes the foundational elements that youth need for success: confidence, literacy, and knowledge of self. Our middle school girls are LEAVES. Leaves are the main energy-conversion section of most plants. Public health research tells us that youth (ten to fourteen years old) are among those most at risk for significant and long-term public health challenges such as obesity. Furthermore, the health practices that youth engage in during these formative years significantly impact their long-term health. The Leaves program, therefore, emphasizes learning and mastering holistic health practices (e.g., anger management, eating and exercise, sexual identity). Our high schoolers are called BRANCHES. As branches grow, a good structure should be established or they will break. Therefore, our teen program enhances girls' self-worth, providing girls the support they need to grow into mature healthy women. The Branches program prioritizes issues of resiliency, planning, cooperation, and goal setting. We have also developed programs specifically for mothers. Like the roots of a tree, mothers provide structural support to their children, but mothers also need support. The ROOTS program equips mothers with skills to help enhance and maintain their own health while attending to the needs of their children.

The work has evolved and GrassROOTS has become a training organization with an emphasis on public health and social justice. The mission of public health is to fulfill society's interest in assuring the conditions by which people can live healthy lives. The mission of social justice is to ensure that all individuals receive fair and equitable treatment as well as access to societal resources including civil, economic, and political liberties. The existing rates of health inequities parallel the social inequities in the society, and the populations who are disproportionately impacted are those who historically have been oppressed and those who are currently struggling for civil and human rights.

When I first started thinking about forming an organization, I gave more attention to the after-school program than the summer component, SuperCamp, but as GrassROOTS grew, the team and I recognized the need to have a summer component. SuperCamp offered an opportunity for more intensive training and allowed us more time to work with and support the girls. My early experience of doing the two types of program separately in two different communities revealed that girls need support year-round. The intensive summer training had a lasting influence on how girls performed throughout the school year.

This strategic learning led us to revise our plan of action for serving girls. We now offer an intensive leadership summer training to girls between the ages of five and fourteen (first through eighth grades, with high school girls as junior camp counselors) and a year-round out-of-school-time program. The curriculum is designed to ground girls in a sense of history and civic responsibility. Our group leaders, many of them educators, work with the girls—and their adult caregivers—to set individual and shared goals and support the girls in meeting their goals over time.

In its current form, each day at SuperCamp begins with a community circle, meditation, and a one-hour walk/run. We include instruction on balanced nutrition, we provide organic fruit and veggies for the girls' snack, and a nutritionist teaches girls and their families about the importance of a healthy diet. Along with doctoral and master's-level scholars, we teach girls sociological issues as well as American and world history, emphasizing the importance of African and African-American contributions. Girls participate in a mentorship series, in which they meet with and learn from professional women trailblazers in the areas of finance, art, science, and technology—the predicted leading industries of the next decade. All girls also learn the fundamentals of body confidence through dance, and girls nine and older learn about sexual health from a clinician and a medical doctor. Our licensed therapist holds weekly sessions with our girls about their mental and emotional health and individual and family sessions with girls and their caregivers. We also take a field trip every Friday. Finally, because we get to see the girls for several years, we work with them to develop and implement social action projects.

Each year we have between twenty and thirty applicants, and based on how many slots are available, we accept four to six new girls into the program. On average, girls enter our program before third grade and return each year for three to five years; they stay with us through their elementary and middle-school years. Once they have completed eighth grade, they can become junior wellness coaches. Those girls and their families who wish to continue undergo a reapplication process, which includes an evaluation and conversation with the SGS (SuperGirls Society) director, a board member, and a camp counselor. In our exchange we lay out what we have observed of the SuperGirl's actions and the extent to which those actions are aligned with the goals and work of the foundation. Our discussion is framed around five core areas of GrassROOTS Leadership and Community Engagement: taking initiative, communication, sharing opinions, demonstrating a desire for excellence, and service and engagement. Furthermore, we ask that each caregiver supply at least two recommendations from other members. The recommendation letter must discuss the caregiver as a community member and rank her top three attributes:

- Eagerness to support
- Kindness toward others
- Optimism
- Responsiveness to my needs and that of my SuperGirl(s)
- Reliability
- Dedication to social justice
- Trustworthiness

Much of our assessment is about the girls, but our observations also include our evaluation of the caregivers in modeling the leadership behavior we demand of the girls and in assessing the extent to which parents are helping their girl and other girls develop into change-makers. We look for evidence of readiness, not just the desire to lead. We measure readiness by examining the ways girls exhibit confidence, self-efficacy, optimism, and entrepreneurialism. Additionally, we look for examples of when girls share opinions and voices with a group. Are they comfortable giving and sharing openly? Do their actions show a willingness to trust members of the community? We also look for demonstrations of the girls' desire for excellence. More specifically, we want to see that girls are willing to push themselves toward their highest potential. Examples include improvement in academic achievement as well as personal goals such as healthy life habits. Moreover, we want to see if girls are actively seeking opportunities to try and master new things. To be able to return, girls and their families must also provide evidence of support from community members. We are looking for examples of an older girl helping a younger one. Similarly, we are looking for cases where caregivers are openly inviting to new caregivers and vice versa. The final criterion concerns service and engagement. All those who wish to return to camp must show that they understand the importance of attending to the needs of the community and giving back to their community by using their gifts and talents to serve others. Girls must complete forty hours of community service and be capable of discussing what they learned from their experiences.

More often than not, we have ample evidence girls could benefit from moving forward in our program. We spend more than sixteen hundred hours with them during the summer and at least one hundred hours throughout the year. However, sometimes the reapplication process becomes contentious, largely because some caregivers become frustrated that we, specifically me, demand too much of the parents and the girls. Some would really prefer to drop their girls off without having to do the things the girls do. "I thought this camp was for the kids; why do I have to do that?" is a common complaint. Some caregivers become frustrated because when they joined the camp they prioritized some matters of personal development over others and are irritated that the girls must develop in multiple areas. For example, in some cases they joined the community hoping their child would become a better public speaker, but are not concerned that their child sometimes lies. Sometimes caregivers are disorganized or busy and will fail to do something, impeding the girls' success. Perhaps caregivers did not read the emails or texts or WhatsApp messages, and their child missed an opportunity to participate in a program activity. Then they want me to overlook those issues and instead focus just on the girl. Sometimes I make allowances for all of these behaviors, but more often than not, I do not. During the interview process and at orientation I explain that if the caregivers cannot model or support the girls, then the program is not a good fit. I repeat and communicate this reality throughout the program and again during these difficult moments. Change-making demands loving support, modeling, and attention. When those things are absent or inconsistent, girls are more likely to underachieve. Change-making is hard. But it is worth it. When girls win, everybody wins.

This emphasis on the whole-self development sometimes leads parents to decide that this camp and program are not a good fit for their girls. This is my favorite group of parents because those parents usually leave cordially. Whether it is the schedule, their girls' new interests, or their own self-realization, these parents usually amicably communicate that, though they like some or all components of the work, they wish for something else. I am delighted by this because, like this book, the work we do has a very specific focus, and I expect that not everyone will enjoy or want to do the required work. It is always better when caregivers identify this mismatch before I do.

The process of reapplication can also highlight the challenge between what I am asking and what parents are willing to do. By the end of the first year of the program, we can see patterns of behaviors that make it clear that some families are not the right fit. This is where contention often rises. By the time the reapplication process begins, I have usually spoken to these caregivers about something I or the team have noted and have asked for some remediation of action. In some instances, I have encouraged caregivers not to reapply, and most will agree. Though infrequent, a few parents do not agree and have reapplied, only to then be confronted with harsh realization and the rehashing of the challenges we have observed. By this time, these caregivers have grown angry or bitter, and some have even written nasty notes. Occasionally I hear angry whispers of folks whose children have come through our program. I do not usually respond to these exchanges, whispers, or notes because I find it unproductive.

Over time, we have grown comfortable with all types of responses because I am aware that what I ask of girls and their families requires an intentionality that is at times uncomfortable and demanding, even irritating. Discomfort is a critical part of growth and change-making, and it is not easy—a point that I repeat several times in this book, that I have repeated at camp, and that cannot be underestimated. However, GrassROOTS' work, my work, has shown that, whether girls are with us for one year or ten, they and their families are transformed and they and the world are made better for having participated in the process.

The experience of deciding that you want to parent like it matters demands an investment in yourself and an investment in your girl. The return on investment is worth it; remember this as you begin taking the strategic action steps to make this possible. Be patient with yourself and with your girl.

The process to get here took a lot of work and patience. I started the journey in 2010 and today SuperCamp has served sixty-five girls and their families in New Jersey—a total of over 150 people— as well as ten girls and parents in Philadelphia. Our after-school programs have served hundreds of girls in middle and high schools in Greensboro, North Carolina; Philadelphia, Pennsylvania; and Newark, New Jersey. The time has come to share our process with the greater community of parents and caregivers out there.

This work was born out of a combination of my own experiences and academic training. I have spent a decade bringing these ideas to life, and this book will serve as a deliberate road map for you, as parents, to raising your own self-realized girls. The strategies I share in *Parent Like It Matters* are the same ones that are the basis of the GrassROOTS' SuperCamp and our SuperGirls Society (SGS). We follow four basic principles of Maat: Truth, Order, Balance, and Reciprocity. These ideas and philosophies are distilled and consolidated from the forty-two laws of an ancient Egyptian faith-based practice call Ma'at. This practice focuses on how we can embrace internal harmony and work to build harmony in the world.

I was inspired by Dr. Sandra Lewis, a psychologist and scholar at Montclair State University and the girls' first yoga instructor, to use this philosophy to guide our work. I was familiar with the principles of Maat, and in 1998 I had even considered changing my last name to Maat. Dr. Lewis's reduction of the principles into four broad categories made them user-friendly, and together she and I along with the GrassROOTS team developed ways to make them practical for our work with girls and their families (see Appendix A). In this book, I refer to internal harmony as "joy" and external harmony as "justice."

These four basic principles provided a sustainable, adaptable framework for joyfulness and change-making. The camp is organized around these four core ideas—and I've organized the book similarly, adapting lessons so that you can embark on this journey with your daughters at home, at your pace, based on your family's needs.

Parts I and II of the book focus on helping you and your girls understand their truths. I outline ways for girls to value themselves and how you as a parent can discover or rediscover who you are and live your truth so that you can be a model for your girl. Parts I and II focus on the principle of TRUTH, which is about honoring the spirit, talents, and abilities that all humans bring to the world. When we practice truth, we are taking a good look at our girls and we are parenting the children we have, not the children we want to have. Embrace of truth allows us to develop a spirit of joy, which begins with gratitude. For us to help our girls see the truth in themselves, however, we must also see the truth about ourselves, regardless of how harsh that may be. The principle of truth runs throughout the book.

Although I offer assignments that you can do alone and with your girl throughout the book, Part III goes into greater depth by asking that you take a strategic approach from the very beginning of your girl's life to make sure that she feels grounded in her culture and heritage. This section utilizes the principle of ORDER that reminds us to honor those who came before us so that we can learn from them in order to grow. Part III also relies on the principle of BALANCE, which teaches us to use our resources wisely. Resources include our knowledge, emotions, friends, and family. When we are in balance we are not overextending or underutilizing the assets we have around us. We are able to make discerning choices among sometimes difficult options.

Finally, Part IV is all about reciprocity. It provides detailed information on how to be reciprocal by sharing our gifts and talents with the world through social action projects. The principle of RECIPROCITY focuses on the practice of both sharing good with others and being grateful. This principle reminds us that a better world happens because we make it so. We practice reciprocity by openly sharing what we have and what we know. Further, if we see gaps in information and resources, we offer to help. We inform and share our activities and accomplishments with the community. We engage in activities that build our communities and improve members' access to resources, and we collaborate to create social good.

The book as a whole takes the perspective that parenting joyful, change-making girls means training and coaching them to become confident, competent, and civic-minded. This is particularly critical for our girls because the world will underestimate them and overlook them every day—even though they will grow up to be women who invest ninety percent of every dollar they earn for the benefit of their families and their communities. A decade of working with these families made me realize it was time to start extending my work with the GrassROOTS families to the larger community. We need all girls to become women who are healthy, who advocate both for themselves and for those with greater needs. We want them to be in the room when philanthropic funds are being allocated, when budgets are being drawn up, when financial aid packages are being negotiated. We want them to disrupt inequity; we want them to work in coalitions to create change; we want them to be the architects of ideas that lead to greater equity in the world. To fulfill these desires, we must start training them *now* to develop a pipeline of change-makers. Regardless of the professions they choose, we want them to see that they can make a positive difference in the world.

Now, you may be surprised to find that this book does not focus solely on your girl. I will frequently ask you to hold the mirror up to yourselves as parents. I will share with you stories of my own and others' pain, healing, and restoration. Why? Because the more I studied the parents around me and their parenting techniques, the more I recognized the effects of the intergenerational transmission of pain, and the more I became obsessive about healing myself. As it turns out, this heal-thyself approach is very important.

Research shows that as parents our past negative experiences can seriously affect how we raise our children. Adversities we faced during childhood do not simply disappear as we age; they become connected to a series of interrelated hardships and stressors that we face as parents. Cumulative science tells us that parents often transfer their distressing symptoms to children. Children can experience secondary trauma when they must depend upon the traumatized person. To break these intergenerational patterns and parent in a way that matters, it is imperative that we as caregivers address issues rooted in childhood trauma and restore ourselves to wholeness.

As the guardian of children, we must ensure that our own private hurts and past heartbreaks don't trip us up without our awareness. This reconciliation is the single most important step toward cultivating in our girls a sense of purpose infused with a spirit of possibility and joy. I believe strongly that we can raise brilliant and resilient girls, even in environments that might feel broken and fundamentally disempowering. However, we can do this only if and when we attend to our past pains and lighten our own emotional loads. We can become powerful examples of self-empowered women who can inspire our girls to become their best selves.

Attending to yourself is the most important part of being a parent. Though you have tremendous power over your children, first you must be able to command yourself. By healing and celebrating yourself, as well as harnessing your joy, you can become who you wish to be.

As parents, your ability to bring about social change is great. You have power each day in the way you parent. You are in charge, particularly in the first ten years of your girl's life. You decide when she sleeps, who is around her, what she watches, and the food she consumes. You are the primary influence on her values, moral reasoning, and ideas, which means you must be ever conscious of what you are modeling for your child. To this end, you must parent like it matters. Start by asking yourself daily:

- What are the values I want to communicate?
- Are my actions aligned with my values?
- Am I setting an example through what I do and say?
- Through the way I behave, do I make my beliefs clear to her?

- What do I need to resolve in myself so that I can parent with joy?

Answers to these questions will help you in your journey of raising a joyful change agent.

But here's the thing: Parenting is not making a cake. And I hesitate to offer prescriptions—or an exact recipe—to you because each family has a unique parenting formula, full of experimentation. I cannot instruct you to add a teaspoon of this and a cup of that to create the child you want. That's because each child has a unique brilliance, and it will take many different attempts to help her discover it.

All I am asking of parents, therefore, is that you do not treat parenting as a strict recipe, or as a chore, but rather recognize that raising a child demands imagination and flexibility. Trust yourself and perhaps have a willingness to creatively adapt the *general guidelines* in this book. I want to share my experiences—both academic and on the ground—so you can be a leader and amplifier for your daughter's personal and social revolution.

Parenting like it matters demands intentionality in the process, not solely a focus on the outcome. The purpose of this book is to get you to think deliberately about the actions you take in your parenting; however, it is critical that you divorce yourself from the suggestion that you can guarantee the outcome. As caregivers, we cannot be certain that our children will be any specific thing—though in truth we wish we could. Instead, we have to focus on making sure we have instilled values, knowledge, competencies, and information so that they can be whatever they want to be.

There will be moments in reading this book and in trying these exercises that you become frustrated with me, with the work, with yourself, and with your child—those feelings are a part of the process. If it makes you feel better to yell a little, that's okay. I am rooting for you and your girl, and I promise that you both will be just fine.

Part I

Who Is Your Girl?

A Look in the Mirror

~~~~~~

> Your children are not your children. They
> are the sons and daughters of life's longing for
> itself. They come through you but not from
> you, and though they are with you yet they
> belong not to you.
>
> —*Kahlil Gibran*

As we undertake this journey with our girls, first we need to understand who they are, on their own terms. If we honor the ways that our girls are uniquely themselves, then both parent and child can gain insight into who she really is and (just as important) who she isn't. Sometimes this is hard because we have our own ideas about who our girls *should* be. Sometimes we think they should be just like us! Other times we think they should be our opposites— *boy, I hope she doesn't turn out like me!* But let's think of Gibran's point above: Raising your girl means honoring her on her terms. Despite the labor it took to bring your girl to the world, once she is outside of your womb she no longer belongs to you. Her presence in the world means she is a sentient being with her own wants and inclinations.

As individuals, children must cultivate and nurture that voice so that they feel capable of expressing opinions with confidence in all areas of their lives. In the early stages, caregivers must therefore attune to their girls' interests and points of view so that they can help the girls grow and value who they are. Research shows that listening to children's wishes and opinions will shape their participation in the family and the world; more specifically, when kids feel that they are heard, they are more likely to share their frustrations and joys with their parents, and they are more likely to be socially integrated at school and in their communities. By listening you are demonstrating to children that they belong and are cared for. Taking the time to listen will help girls understand the important distinction between adults who look after them and those who actually care for them.

Caring begins with listening.

Listening to what your child wants and reconciling her desires with your own wishes is important for building a stable bond between you and for creating a fuller expression of her. However, listening and caring does not mean granting your girl's every wish. Instead, it means as caregivers and parents we must develop strategies for attending to her wishes—all while guiding her to make healthy choices. Negotiating and achieving this balance between our girls' requests and our responsibilities as guardians can be difficult. Often it means making hard choices—as well as helping her see the value in you rejecting her wants. She may want the latest pair of sneakers, but her feet are still growing each month. You can and should say no without any regret. She may want to spend the night at a friend's house during the school week, but that will interfere with her sleep schedule. You should say no. Don't worry: Becoming familiar and comfortable with *no* is good for her. She will be okay. But note that your refusal must be thoughtfully made and conveyed. It must first begin with listening to and hearing your girl's ideas and opinions. Let her make her case. Hearing her point of view will give you insight into the logic she is using to make decisions and assess situations. Ask her to listen to the arguments that you lay out because she needs to become familiar with your point of view. Trust me, this will come in handy for the future. The more she knows about your perspective, the more she will be able to discern what things you value and do not value—and vice versa.

This reciprocal understanding will facilitate your relationship and bring you closer. Decision-making then becomes a process of thoughtful consideration born out of dialogue. If we listen to our girls, then when we have to draw the line on some things, they will be more likely to understand and/or accept our decision. But the work begins with listening and exchanging ideas.

Parent-child communication—both form and content—is critically important for youth development. The way parents communicate with their children can impact the kids' emotional competency and self-esteem. Scholars have found that parents explaining events and emotions clearly has been linked with higher self-esteem in their children. Furthermore, when parents and children collaboratively discuss and make meaning about children's experiences, it enhances self-esteem.

However, listening to our children and accepting their ideas is sometimes difficult, especially when we have our own perception of who they are or what they *should* want. Too often, in an effort to balance a fear that outsiders may perceive that we overindulge our children, some of us reflexively balk at our daughters' desires.

For example, I strongly advise against caregivers choosing celebratory moments like birthdays to teach or train children about self-control and character development. These are not the ideal moments for such action. Choose, instead, everyday moments as opportunities to help your girl recognize her resources and privileges so that she can practice good decision-making.

A constant repetition of "no" will not help her make good choices. "No, you cannot have this game. No, you cannot get those shoes. No, you cannot go to that event" will not teach her why those choices may not be appropriate. Consider asking her to share her plan for how and why she wants to do something. Provide her with a few probing questions about her plan and then ask her to describe the pros and cons of her choices. Explain to her that her plan and decision must not demand your time or money. She must use only the resources that she has available to her. Example: If you go to the game on a school night, how will you get there? Who will come and pick you up? Have you completed all your other obligations including homework? What time do you expect to get back?

Having a lot of material resources will not satisfy her most insatiable desires. Still, it's important to understand the sources and natures of her desires. Acknowledge what she craves, so that you can recognize her in ways that are meaningful to her, not just to you. Do not simply give her what you wish to give, but rather give her, within reason, what *she* wishes to receive. Respond in her love language. Too often parents want their children to acquiesce to their wishes without considering their children's perspective. This oversight can make your girl feel like her ideas and feelings do not matter, or worse, are less important than yours. Hear the way your girl wants to be celebrated and honored. Give priority to her requests. Recognize and separate yourself from her.

Take the case of Nadine and Patrice.

One of our GrassROOTS SuperGirls, Patrice, had always wanted a birthday party with lots of friends, but her mother, Nadine, did not honor her wishes, choosing instead to host intimate events in her backyard. Nadine often invited few of Patrice's friends because she wanted the party to be convenient and easy for her to execute. She did not negotiate with her daughter or her daughter's friends and their parents about attending, and as a result there were often more adults than children in attendance, the majority of whom were Nadine's friends. There was no dancing or children's games. All activities—with the exception of cake cutting—were held outdoors. The whole event would be wrapped up before nightfall when caregivers picked up their children.

Nadine hadn't had birthday parties herself as a child, so she didn't see the big deal in these celebrations. In fact, she found birthday parties to be ostentatious and financially wasteful. She prided herself on the fact that she was not one of those parents who threw lavish celebratory events. Each year she planned the party by herself with little input from Patrice. Although Patrice could select some of the friends she wanted to attend, Nadine made the final decision.

I was always among those invited, so I got a chance to see the parties for many years. They were always nice; the adults had a great time. We watched movies, ate food, and drank mixed beverages. The kids seemed happy enough in the backyard, and everyone indulged in cake.

I didn't learn how Patrice felt about these parties until I asked what she would be doing for her ninth birthday, which was just around the corner. She told me that for years she had asked her mom to plan a proper birthday party with lots of friends, but her mom had simply disregarded her opinion, opting instead to hold the usual festivities. Saddened by Patrice's story, I talked with Nadine about her daughter's request.

Nadine was frustrated by the idea that she would have to coordinate such a large event. As a busy working mother, she felt that she did not have time for party planning. Furthermore, she was frugal and did not want to spend what she felt was an excessive amount of money on a child's birthday party. I asked her how much her annual birthday party budget was. She spent roughly five hundred dollars each birthday. To me that felt like a hefty sum. Actually, most of the funds were spent on the adults who ate and drank. Significantly fewer dollars were spent on the kids who ate pizza and cake.

My conversations with Nadine revealed that she did not want Patrice to have a birthday party because she wanted her child to see the triviality of parties. Nadine hoped that Patrice would learn to devalue such things and assumed that if she deprived Patrice of parties, then she would wean her off the idea. Her plan backfired. The more Patrice did not have a party, the more she wanted one.

In fact, what was celebratory to Nadine did not have much value for Patrice. The cerebral child that Nadine was hoping to cultivate was indeed academically talented, but she was also artistically driven—and she *loved* parties. She yearned for a party so she could put on a show for friends. She saw her birthday as the perfect opportunity.

But the thought of a showcase annoyed Nadine; she felt it was pretentious and unnecessary. The vision she had for her child was of a demure and reserved girl. But much to Nadine's chagrin, Patrice was not that girl. In fact, she was quite different. Patrice had been yearning for the theater and the stage. She had a strong desire to be seen and heard. She wanted and loved the spotlight.

I encouraged Nadine to hire an event planner and pool funds from family and friends to host a birthday party for Patrice. Reluctantly, she agreed. When Nadine finally heard how Patrice wanted to be celebrated, she was able to create for her a beautiful ninth birthday—a pop theme in which she and her four closest friends dressed up as the Spice Girls. With all eyes on her, Patrice got to play the role of Scary Spice, rapping and dancing to "Wannabe," their most popular song.

The audience cheered, and Patrice was never happier.

That afternoon, Patrice felt celebrated because her mom finally understood and granted her wish. By embracing her daughter's love of performance, Nadine was validating her child's authentic self.

A year after that watershed birthday party, with her mother's blessing, Patrice auditioned for a theater company, earning a few parts in local plays. Today, at sixteen, Patrice has participated in several school performances and is active in her school's theater club. Indeed, Nadine has become quite a theater-mom, serving as the president of the boosters for Patrice's drama club. The party had opened Nadine's eyes to who her daughter was.

While celebrating Patrice's birthday the way she wanted was Nadine's opportunity to prioritize her daughter's wishes, valuing and celebrating your girl does not demand a birthday, specific achievement, or occasion. It is about being acknowledged and recognized simply because she exists. Most important, it is about listening to her and tending to her emotional and physical needs so that she feels safe and loved. As a caregiver, providing that feeling of being safe and loved must be among your primary charges because it so deeply shapes her sense of self-concept, namely the way she sees herself and the impact she perceives she can make on the world.

According to psychologist Abraham Maslow, beyond the need

for basic physical safety, the need "to love and to be loved" is fundamentally important for people's emotional safety. Scholars agree that what matters to us, beyond our mere existence, is the explicit confirmation that we exist and that our existence alone—sans any specific achievement—is a wonderful thing.

In essence, such theorists are making clear that feeling loved for simply being alive and being who we are affirms us and therefore brings us joy. My husband, Scott, and I have always made a conscious effort to parent our daughter, Marley, with this tenet in mind, ensuring that Marley knows she is loved. For us this began with letting her know her origin story. It is a simple story: Her dad wanted to have a child—me, not so much. But after several years of prodding, eventually my love for him persuaded me to become a mother, even though we were stretched thin financially.

Marley was born on a cold January morning at University of Pennsylvania Hospital, eleven days after I defended my dissertation and became Dr. Janice Johnson Dias. We were elated. I was now a doctor, and our financial situation was looking up. In a few short months, I was going to leave unemployment and the city of Philadelphia behind for a handsome stipend and a professional development budget at the University of Michigan at Ann Arbor. But before that could happen, I had to figure out how to be a mom to this baby girl without family support. Scott and I were ignorant of what to do. However, we were determined to do the one thing we felt we could do right: We were going to just love her and make sure she knew that we did.

As Marley became older, we used every opportunity we could to let her know that she was the living embodiment of our love. She was born out of love and surrounded by love. As often as she would allow us, we shared with her how excited our friends and family were about her birth, so much so that they organized baby showers in multiple cities. Now, at sixteen years old, she has the evidence of all that love in the journal of wishes people made for her at her biggest baby shower. Each birthday she reads it as a reminder of how much she is loved.

In many respects, our parenting practices adopted sociologist and psychologist Erich Fromm's basic elements of love: care, respect, knowledge, and responsibility. We did, however, adopt these ideas to address the patriarchy and bio-determinism embedded in his theory. Unlike Fromm, we did not assume that children can form a core attachment only to their mothers, and we rejected the concept that mothers are the single best caregivers of children. We made room for the multiple forms of attachment (i.e., to our close friends, teachers, and both parents) that were necessary for our daughter to thrive.

As much as possible we have broken free from some of the traditional gender norms that organize many households; her dad took her on playdates with other mothers while I took her to sporting events. He was as much responsible for making her dinner as I was. Even at times when she was yearning for just her mommy, we reminded her that she had two parents available to her. Scott was pushed to wake up in the middle of the night to attend to her fevers and nosebleeds. (Why should I be the only one who lost sleep?) In her early years, she did not simply run to me for the bottle, or food, or hugs because I was Mom. Each of us had a baby bag: Mine was black; his was camouflage. She was equally and differently attached to both of us. Together, we worked hard to ensure she knew that she was cared for and that her care was not simply the responsibility of one person but rather the shared responsibility of both caregivers.

From very early on, we pushed her to acknowledge and be happy with her own success. Whether learning to walk or swim or mastering a new word, we pushed her to be happy with her own effort and achievement. We were and are always happy to praise her, but we wanted her to learn the art of being pleased with her own success. We would say, "Great job, Marley" and ask her to repeat the phrase. When she was very young it sounded weird. She almost seemed to be talking to an unknown third person, but as she got older, she would repeat it out loud, "Great job, Marley," and over time she began to recognize that she was Marley. Our hope was that these self-congratulatory messages would become her inner voice. By the time she was five or six years old, before praising her we would ask her, "How do you feel about how you did?" The goal was for her to understand how she was assessing her own effort and achievements. This process taught us a lot. We learned that she had a tendency to be hard on herself, and but she could also praise others. We also discovered that she had great respect for the feelings and needs unique to other persons.

It has been remarkable to see Marley's confidence in herself grow over the years. Now a teenager, Marley has become an activist and author. In 2018, she wrote a book: *Marley Dias Gets It Done and So Can You.* The book, written from her perspective, outlines her journey of creating and leading the #1000BlackGirlBooks campaign and her desire to diversify children's literature. At ten years old, she was frustrated that the books she was reading in school lacked diverse characters. Driven by the desire to expand the curriculum, she set out to collect one thousand books in which Black girls were the main characters. Her campaign met with great success; by 2019, she had collected over twelve thousand books and donated them to individuals, schools, businesses, and community organizations that needed them.

A few years ago, Marley did a big TED-style talk at the Boston Convention and Exhibition Center for the organization Inbound. She was going to be on the same platform as Serena Williams and other megastars. Sadly, I was extremely busy at the time with teaching and GrassROOTS and could not give her the time and attention I ordinarily did. She had to write the talk by herself and rehearse with the publicist. Though I read through her initial comments, I would not see the final talk until the day she gave it. She titled the talk "Do Your Best, Don't Worry About Being the Best." In this twelve-minute speech, she said: "In my family . . . we don't compare. We focus within. We work on being our best self daily. We work on giving our best at everything we do. We strive to be the best version of who we are." This work of focusing attention on the self is a critical part of the way we have taught her to understand love.

But the self needs others; therefore, being loving demands respect for others. More specifically, it means making a conscientious effort never to exploit others. Perhaps you are wondering how young kids could be exploitive. Well, kids can form friendships based on superficial values. Early on, we realized it was important for Marley to learn not to make friends only with the kids who had the best computer gadget, biggest house, or best birthday party. It was important to us that she forge relationships based on mutual respect and that she never exploit another person as a means to an end. For us, exploitation demonstrates a deficiency in character and a lack of love. If you're worried about navigating this issue, don't worry. In the final section of the book, I discuss these issues in greater detail.

We have been clear in our parenting practice that love is not an idea. Love can be best understood through our actions. Love is about showing up, listening, remembering, and being there for others. We taught Marley about love in the biblical way my grandmother explained it to me: "Love is patient; love is kind. It does not envy, it does not boast, it is not proud. It does not dishonor others, it is not self-seeking, it is not easily angered, it keeps no record of wrongs. Love does not delight in evil but rejoices with the truth. It always protects, always trusts, always hopes, always perseveres" (1 Corinthians 13:4–8).

My hope is that this framework for love helps her to understand that our devotion to her is endless and is made visible not only in our words, but also in our actions. Love is in the tangible things like providing a home, clothing, and food, but it is also in listening to her, asking her about her day, and learning her various new dance moves. All of these actions are our deliberate ways of showing our love.

Research on love suggests that just because caregivers perform these actions does not mean children will experience them the way we want them to; however, it does increase the likelihood that they will. And when children feel love, the rewards are great. Feeling loved actually builds brain development. Scholars argue that feeling attached to and connected to caregivers is crucial for the development of brain pathways, such that these connections promote emotional strength and self-regulation in children. Psychologists Erica

Burman and Majia Holmer Nadesan found that early, ample, and appropriate parental stimulation is critically important for the optimal development of children's brains and future intellectual capacity. Attention and one-on-one time with caregivers can wire children's brains in positive ways and promote emotional attachment. This type of emotional connection, namely feeling loved, is a safety net that builds resilience. Building resilience supports children's emotional capabilities and facilitates self-confidence and cheerful adaptability—what we might call joyfulness.

In his *Art of Loving*, Fromm also argues that feeling loved reduces the sense of isolation and instills in the child a love for living, which gives her the feeling that it is good to be alive. Having an emotional safety net, such as the feeling of being loved, is dually protective; in some instances, children can call on that resource when they need it, and at other times it is a dependable and predictable resource that anchors children. This anchoring allows them to feel safe taking risks—another key quality in raising a changemaker.

ASSIGNMENTS

Make a mirror that reflects your girl.

Purchase a mirror at your local store and, together with your girl, write three or four major adjectives that describe her. Tape those adjectives on the mirror so that they can serve as a constant reflection and reminder of who she really is.

Practice becoming an active listener.

Active listening is a way of listening and responding to another person that improves mutual understanding. As a reminder, hearing is not listening. To adequately listen, you must stop what you're doing.

Sit down so that you can be at your girl's level. Make eye contact with her. Let her finish her sentences at her own pace. It may be hard for children to find the correct words to use, so be patient.

Help boost her self-confidence.

One of the foremost ways to bolster self-confidence is through trying new things and gaining mastery of them. Nothing is more powerful than having a direct experience of mastery to increase self-efficacy. In cases where girls cannot engage in a particular action, the next best option is observing people around them, especially people they consider role models.

Help your girl identify the attributes that she believes can propel her forward and ask her to visualize herself behaving successfully.

At SuperCamp, we ask our girls to study a notable person. Our instructions demand that each girl outline the attributes she admires about the person and make a Venn diagram of the attributes she has in common with this person. The research means that she must learn more than the superficial details about the person's life. She must review film, read interviews, and even get autobiographical information on the person to understand what they were like as children. In our experience, we have found that notable people are almost always asked about their greatest accomplishments and their measures of success. Each year it is exciting to watch as the girls discover that even these famous folks do not define themselves simply by their external achievements.

Sitting together, make a list of the qualities of someone your girl deems successful and then line up her own qualities next to that, so she can see the connection, the crossover, the possibility.

Tell her, remind her, and show her that she is loved.

Many of us tell our children daily that we love them. Sometimes it is a quick "I love you" before rushing off to work or hanging up the phone. These moments are important, but they are not enough. Show your girl with your daily actions that she is loved and cared for; it will help her feel safe and worthy.

- Write her a handwritten note and put it next to her breakfast.
- Send her a midday text message of you singing her favorite song. At the end of her school day she will enjoy your song.
- Draw her a picture that expresses how you feel about her.
- Do little unexpected somethings that share your feelings of love for her.

2

A Spirit of Joy

~~~~~~

> Joy is the infallible sign of the presence of
> God.
> —*Pierre Teilhard de Chardin*

> I define joy as a sustained sense of well-being
> and peace, a connection to what matters.
> —*Oprah Winfrey*

When people meet my daughter, Marley, they're often impressed by how articulate and bright she is, but what surprises them even more is her joy. She has a delightful and lighthearted spirit—despite being in the business of trying to create social change. The typical image of a social change activist is a person who labors under the weight of the world's inequities, or someone who is so fiercely passionate that their animated self resembles anger. But Marley has grown into a *joyful* change-maker.

While we often talk about wanting our kids to be happy, we don't spend nearly enough time thinking about *joy,* a much more valuable emotion. What's the difference? For some philosophers, happiness is hedonistic and temporary; joyfulness, on the other hand, is a choice to exist and *act* in a kind of enlightened state of being beyond our immediate moment. Considered by Spinoza and Nietzsche as the feeling of becoming more active in the world, joyfulness emphasizes the embodied connection between self and world. Being joyful is about experiencing more than temporary enjoyment; it goes far beyond contentment. Joy is about the attitudes we have toward life—it comes from within and is linked to *action*. Joy is also about connection and self-power. Spinoza argues that joy is the feeling of an increase in one's powers to affect things; therefore, joy is inseparable from the actualization of power. It is the feeling of becoming more active in the world or, to put it differently, of becoming part of a bigger world which one participates in organizing and creating change.

Achieving joyfulness is about refining and even rewriting the very nature with which we were born so that we can become who we wish to be. It requires a particular attitude, one that is always appreciative of life and those around us. It demands a set of actions that facilitate equity, ensuring that the world around us allows others to become who they wish. Translation: To reach this joy, we must have a sense of gratefulness, respect for human rights, and a desire to engage in actions that can bring about social change.

Though joyful people can experience emotions like sadness, disappointment, or anger, those will be transient moments in the larger arc of their lives. Joyful people have a reservoir of positivity and optimism that they tap when challenges come their way. With internal peace, we can move through the world with hope, understanding that negative emotions do not have to become defining characteristics. Instead, our lives are driven by a structured and positive attitude that infuses the spirit and is inextricably woven through everything we do. Therefore, we use anger, frustration, sadness, fear, and other negative emotions as catalysts for purposeful action. To quote my daughter, "Frustration is a fuel that leads to the development of an innovative and useful idea." Joyful people see this, know this, and act accordingly.

This choice to act is precisely what change-making is about—and change-making is joyful. But this mindset doesn't occur on its own. We must feel agentic and emboldened enough to act. We must also feel safe—safe to make mistakes, safe to speak our minds, and safe to invent worlds. Only then can we provide a strong yet pliable framework within ourselves and our children, especially our girls, to address the inequities that we see.

The process of cultivating a spirit of joy demands attending to what is inside of us as well as addressing those things that are outside and around us. It means recognizing and knowing who we are. Developing or harnessing joyfulness, then, is about tapping into the best of ourselves to find tranquility and calm even, and especially, during challenging times. Adopting a joyful perspective allows us to distinguish between and manage how we respond to executing the necessities of life (things that we must do) and self-defining activities (things that enrich our spirits). This framework of joyfulness can replenish rather than drain us, even when we are performing our daily mundane tasks like shopping, homework assignments, soccer games, and bill paying. It protects us from feeling disquieted and worn down.

In this book I tackle joy early on, because much of what follows depends on these ideas, specifically the interrelationship of joy, gratefulness, and equity. I am asking you to engage in being internally serene while also teaching your children about difficult and disruptive social issues. Some people may believe that being joyful and being socially conscious are at odds. They may assume that a person, especially a child, who is aware of the inequities of the world cannot be joyful, and that an understanding of racism, sexism, homophobia, debt, and other frustrations and inequities will burden a child and steal her joy. But joy cannot be stolen. That's because joy is self-created by our own work.

Being joyful also means that we feel connected to the world around us. We must feel related to our neighbors, our communities, and our schools. This sense of connectedness, which may at times make us feel vulnerable, is precisely what we need to create and live a peaceful life. It is this same dedication that allows us to advocate for and embolden our children to fight for greater equity in the world.

I have not always felt connected to the world around me. At times, being an immigrant from a rural community who finds herself living in cosmopolitan cities has made me feel out of place.

However, despite this outward disconnection, I have often felt grounded in exactly who I am.

One of the ways to make joy the center of our lives is to be present in our lives, constantly evaluating, reframing, and transforming the way we engage with life, specifically the world around us. Through my years of sociology and public health research, and through working with the girls and their families at GrassROOTS, I have learned that self-assessment is a necessary meditative process that invites significant internal peace and a deep sense of well-being. Meditation doesn't only mean we sit and deeply reflect on our lives; it also means that we consistently conduct appraisals of ourselves. Those evaluations can happen anywhere and at any time. But appraisal demands that we stay informed, connected, and committed to leading a fully conscious life.

The challenge for so many of us is that we want to unconsciously move about the world. We want to shut out all the unpleasant things that are happening in and around us, particularly if those things are upsetting (e.g., police violence, homelessness, crime, social inequality, health crises). But achieving internal peacefulness cannot happen if we shut down uncomfortable realities or emotions. Rather, we must invite the world and those truths into our daily conversations and thoughts. We must know and think about how what is happening in the outside world affects how we feel and act. We must live an integrated life at emotional and social levels. By becoming informed, invested, and engaged in what occurs in the world, we can gain greater understanding and empathy for the victims and even the perpetrators of inequity. Increasing our empathy will allow us to respond in ways that facilitate social connectedness.

Also, integration of social identities and information is helpful because it is efficient. Though there is a conventional push to compartmentalize our emotions and identities, I am suggesting an alternative course of action. Why? When we categorize or separate our emotions and self into tiny pieces, we diminish our wholeness. In essence, that type of action can create fabricated personas that are quite time-consuming to maintain. For example, it is reasonable to put some things off until you can adequately manage them; however, it is unwise to put off certain emotions. Further, it may even prove damaging to present one-dimensional versions of yourself in hopes of creating boundaries. We must do as Nobel Prize winner and author Doris Lessing suggests in her book *The Golden Notebook:* "We must not divide things off, must not compartmentalize." She argues that we ought to be "Bound. Free. Good. Bad. Yes. No. Capitalism. Socialism. Sex. Love. . . ." We should embrace ourselves and the things around us openly.

There is ample psychological research to support this course of action. Scholars tell us that people with overdeveloped compartmentalized emotions, who separate positive and negative self-beliefs into distinct self-aspects, do not thrive in life. Such individuals often find themselves performing for others, switching identities to fit into the varied worlds of which they are a part, feeling like imposters in each one. For example, if persons consistently seek positive statements about themselves in order to maintain a positive mood and high self-esteem, they may not have the resiliency to handle negative statements. Further, when those negative feelings or commentaries arise, individuals may be flooded with negative self-beliefs, and this can lead to dramatic mood swings. In contrast, knowing and blending positive and negative self-beliefs can create more stable moods and greater stability. This intermixing of emotions can help us be the leader-parents we wish to be. By showing our fully integrated selves, we are showing our daughters that they may embrace all aspects of their selves, both the positive and the negative, to be a complicated whole.

At SuperCamp we spend a lot of time working to get girls and caregivers comfortable showing their innermost and gleeful selves. For the youngest group of girls, our Seedlings (first through third grade), this is easy. They are often uninhibited when they arrive at our doorstep. They say what is on their minds. They can freely articulate their likes and dislikes, much to their parents' chagrin. Oftentimes parents have hopes—stated or unstated—that we will actually bridle some of their youthful energies. I sometimes feel bad when they discover that what we really do is multiply that energy and redirect it.

Whereas the Seedlings are free, our middle schoolers are very different. Many arrive guarded and even surreptitious. They often present their performative rather than honest selves. On the first day of camp, their parents are around; therefore, they adopt whatever dominant identity they believe their parents want to see. If they believe their parents see them as artists, then they show their artistic selves—laughing and dancing. If their parents see them as studious, then they will refer to a book they are reading and their love for learning.

In the afternoon, after their parents have left, they have lots of time to free play. During their free time, they can play by themselves or with others. They can choose a game, a book, or art supplies, talk to the counselors, play music, or even just lie on a mat. It is always curious to watch them decide what to do. On day one, almost all of them will find one or two persons to hang out with. They will almost all just sit and talk, often looking out to see if the counselors are watching. Concerned about our watchful eyes, everyone "behaves" themselves and does as expected.

Over time they become less concerned about governance and more willing to express the things that make them happy. It is interesting to watch them do things in dyads and in large groups. Girls start to invent activities that utilize the talents of everyone. Someone will sing as they enter their invented massage parlor. Smaller and younger girls will walk on the backs of bigger girls as they enter the parlor. The girls who like math will count the fake money. Other girls who like art will make the signs for their created lobbies. It is during these unguided moments that we discover what the girls do and do not like.

As time passes, we begin to see the weight of the performance-self diminish among middle-school girls. They begin to act more freely, even silly. For parents this can sometimes seem like a regression because their once-constrained daughters seem more childlike. We encourage this childlike gleefulness because it is energizing. Unencumbered by the rules, middle-school girls become more expressive.

A major downside for parents is that this period often coincides with girls becoming more expressive in all areas of their lives. So, the girl who was once compliant may now express a lack of desire for and interest in some activities. Girls will reveal to their parents that they don't like the sport chosen for them or the person who hangs out at their house or the food served for dinner.

It can all be a bit much. It is at this point that parents text or call me often with complaints, such as "She told me, 'Dr. Janice says I should say how I feel.'" As irritated as the parents sometimes are, I am always pleased, and I am convinced the parents are as well. Creating an environment in which girls can be unbridled and free gives us access into what brings them the most joy.

And for us to achieve harmony in ourselves and in the world, we must be honest about who we are. Joy relies on acknowledging the truths about ourselves.

During the first week of SuperCamp, girls learn about the principle of truth. We emphasize that all human beings have their own unique talents and abilities that they bring to the world, and we must honor those things in others and in ourselves. At SuperCamp, we use poetry, cultural studies, creative expression, and education to support girls' full expression of their own gifts, talents, and abilities. We also make it a practice to speak truth and do the right thing, even when no one is watching.

Truth in action therefore means we share our ideas and thoughts with each other, openly and honestly considering each other's perspective. We develop authentic relationships with each other, including our parents, and give each other the benefit of the doubt. We cheer for others when they succeed. The act of celebrating ourselves, showing our authentic selves rather than our performing selves, helps us live in our truth.

It is this revelation that leads our girls to become more expressive and more joyful. Take Terri. From our first meeting she was captivating. She was a tall girl with the presence and grace of a supermodel. Her clothes were stylish, her coils were immaculately laid, and her costume jewelry was bright and well-coordinated with her nails and leggings. Her mom, Traci, was an adult version—equally ostentatious and bold in her clothing. They attended our community information session. They had read everything on the website, were prepared for the on-site interview, and were accepted into the camp.

On the first day, they came with matching outfits. Terri was articulate and seemingly self-assured. She didn't laugh much, barely spoke to any other girls, and stuck by her mother's side for the first half of the day. As an only child who went to a small Quaker school, she was very comfortable talking to adults and the one other girl she knew, but she seemed slightly apprehensive about engaging with others. During the free periods, she sat by herself with her book. It was clear to everyone that she was bright, but it was hard to discover more about her. The same was true of her mother, who did not talk much with the other parents. The first week went by, and Terri remained reserved. At the end of the first week during community circle, we asked her what she had learned about the principle of truth. She said she had discovered that it was okay to be smart. The answer was fine, but it felt incomplete, as if she had more ideas but was not yet ready to share.

The team and I discussed how we would help her reveal more of herself. The more we know about the girls, the more we can support them in their development. All middle-school girls are partnered with a younger girl. We partnered her with one of the most high energy girls—Tara, an athletic and energetic eight-year-old. Unlike Terri, Tara found it challenging not to laugh at almost everything. She was easily distracted, and she loved to perform. Whether on a field trip or at the campsite, we asked that Terri spend time with Tara. The look of displeasure on her face assured us that this was a great match. Often girls want to be partnered with someone similar to themselves rather than someone who complements them. The team agreed that Tara's exuberance was a perfect complement for Terri's more reserved persona.

Though there were clear moments of frustration on each of their parts over the first two weeks, they rubbed off on each other. Tara began to focus a bit more during lectures, and Terri started to dance and sing. By the third week of camp, we couldn't stop the formerly reticent Terri from singing and dancing. She was often found in fits of laughter. Indeed, she had even made some new friends. Outside of Tara, she found comfort with other equally erudite girls who also liked to sing and dance. Without much outward discussion on our parts, Terri became a bit of a social butterfly.

Too often we pit intellectual aptitude against other forms of genius, and in so doing we run the risk of stymieing childlike behaviors. Terri's ability to embrace levity did not diminish her academic strengths; in fact, it may have added to them. At the end of camp she performed a poem she wrote to the group. There was not a dry eye in the room. The emotion she expressed revealed a self that had grown beyond the formerly stoic girl who had entered camp. She was more joyful.

Joyfulness comes from the ability to show the various parts of ourselves, which requires that we integrate our thoughts, beliefs, and actions. Research in positive psychology tells us that becoming socially integrated is vitally important to our mental health and our tranquility. What does "socially integrated" mean, you may ask? Being social! Having friends. Seeking the company of others. Reaching out to others to provide help, comfort, support. All that good stuff. In the context of raising joyful change-making girls, it means that it is important for our girls to achieve that social integration by connecting with others, avoiding social isolation, and *volunteering.*

Social psychologists agree that benefits of volunteering are multifold, that volunteerism not only enhances life satisfaction, but also helps build self-esteem, gives us a sense of control over life, improves our physical health, and reduces depression. Helping others can also, quite simply, put us in a good mood and distract us from our own stressors. So, in addition to benefiting others when we volunteer, it's good for our well-being, for our sense of self, and for the world.

Volunteerism asks that we give to others. Though some will see volunteering as an unselfish act, at GrassROOTS we recognize that we always get more by giving. Girls are required to volunteer forty hours per year. About half of these hours are organized by the foundation, and the other half must be organized by the girls and their families. Only those who complete their volunteer hours are eligible to return to camp each year. The principle of reciprocity that organizes our work demands that girls and their families demonstrate a clear understanding and commitment that each of us must give back to the world. We demand that girls share the resources they have and also show gratitude. This principle reminds us that a better world happens because we make it so. At Super-Camp we enter into a partnership with girls, their parents, and our partners. These individuals bring talents, commitment, and financial and emotional resources. Therefore, we give back to them by saying thank you to all those who give of themselves to us. We openly share what we have and know. If we see gaps in information and resources, we offer to help. We also engage in activities that build our communities and improve members' access to resources. Volunteerism, as we practice it, allows us to build communities through social relationships and connection.

For some girls this is particularly difficult. Take Beth, who in her own words finds it "hard to connect with people I don't know." When she first started at GrassROOTS she was six years old and struggled to interact with people, choosing instead to hang onto her mother's leg. While other girls served bread at the soup kitchen, carried drinks to the elders, or danced with participants at the turkey giveaway, Beth shied away. When she was not with her mother, she could be found hiding in a corner with her book. Despite the consistent teaching about the value of sharing ourselves with others, Beth struggled in expressing her thoughts, ideas, and feelings. On multiple occasions she would barely make her volunteer hours. The team met with her family because we were concerned that she was not understanding the principle of reciprocity, one of the defining parts of our work. Beth insisted that she understood, but couldn't fully articulate why she was unable to volunteer. Reluctantly, she completed her forty hours each year.

After a few years, Beth's attitude toward volunteering started to change. Each summer, twice a week, SuperGirls read Black girl books to kindergarteners. During camp, girls practice their read-alouds. Each visit, two different SuperGirls are selected to read. Because of her love for reading, we asked Beth to help the girls practice their read-alouds. She was delighted with her new leadership role. She was even more excited to be the first reader. Whereas she was reluctant to volunteer at the soup kitchen and community garden, reading to kindergarteners made her very happy. But she still struggled. After four years, she finally shared that volunteering had been so hard because she has difficulty connecting to people she does not know. So to help her, we gave her some guiding questions that she could ask of unfamiliar people. These open-ended questions help create conversations. My absolute favorite conversation starter is "Tell me about yourself." This inquiry is a call to action that invites people to share things that are most important to them. In November 2019, we were able to witness Beth try this new approach with elders at the housing development in Newark where GrassROOTS consistently volunteers. It made all the difference. She laughed and danced with senior citizens for hours. Her newfound confidence that it is okay to talk to people led her back to her love, reading. She has recently started volunteering at the local YMCA, where she is reading stories to preschoolers.

For caregivers wondering how to get their children to value volunteering, consider the following suggestions for creating a positive experience for you and your child:

- Volunteer together. You must model for them ways to give and care for others.
- Lean into their loves. Ask them how they think they can support others and where they wish to volunteer.
- Commit to a specific issue and location. The consistency of

going to the same location helps you and your girl connect with individuals. This will reduce the impersonalized or tourism nature of many volunteer opportunities.

- Make it a routine. Consistency will help make volunteering a part of a family practice and build the foundation for being a change-maker. Going at the same time each week or month will make it a regular part of your family's life. For GrassROOTS SuperGirls, volunteerism is an organizational imperative, but we encourage you to make it a family goal to give of yourself each month. Using a calendar, decide what activities you as a family will do each month. Choose a day or date that works best for you. It could be every other Sunday or Saturday, even Wednesday evenings. Routinize your volunteer time so that as other activities arise, it doesn't get lost. Here again, I suggest you develop a family calendar of regular events and add your volunteerism to it. Below is a list of major causes by month; you can organize around these or others, many of which can be found online.

January: Martin Luther King Day of Service

February: World Day of Social Justice/Black History Month

March: Global Recycling Day/Women's History Month

April: National Volunteer Month/World Book Day

May: Mental Health Awareness Month/World No Tobacco Day

June: Race for the Cure/World Environment Day

July: Juvenile Arthritis Awareness Month

August: Habitat for Humanity

September: International Literacy Day/September 11 National Day of Service and Remembrance

October: National Bullying Prevention Month/World Food Day

November: World Kindness Day/Thanksgiving

December: World AIDS Day/Toys for Tots

- Educate and debrief about giving experiences. Spend some time before participating in an activity discussing why you volunteer, how to behave while volunteering, and why this place or issue matters. After the experience, always talk with your girl about what she learned while volunteering. More specifically, ask her what she has learned about herself. It is important that she is able to recognize that she is not just giving but also getting.

ASSIGNMENTS

Commit to joy.

Grab a piece of paper and write down: *I will live a joyful life*. Then post that in the most visible place in your home. Keep in mind that being joyful is a matter of daily intention and willful action. Every day, look at that piece of paper and remind yourself why it is important to you and to your child. By cultivating a spirit of joy within yourself, you are ideally positioned to embolden your girl to live the same way. Remember, you are her example of joy personified.

Laugh more.

Joy is about levity and bringing a lighter spirit to all you do. Levity creates a sense of inner peacefulness. The supermarket, back-to-school nights, even athletic games are ripe for comedic adventures. Instead of dreading these things, consider embracing them to find the treasured moments of real brightness. Playfulness is often dismissed as childish. But when we are young, joy seems accessible and easy to achieve. Laughing revives that memory.

   The intensive daily work of being a parent and provider can

feel routine, like drudgery—cooking, housekeeping, transporting your children to and from places that they need to be, working a job to keep everyone afloat. It's often the same thing, day in and day out. So how do you find the joy?

- Add music to everything you do. Any kind of music will do. If you love it, that is all that matters. Going to the supermarket or the mall, even the doctor's office, grab your ear pod or headphones and listen to some music as you shop.
- If possible, shop when the store first opens and no one is around, so you can dance through the aisles.
- Get to your child's sporting event early and park where you can see the field. Use the time in the car to catch up on your favorite audiobook or radio program before the game.
- Wake up before everyone else rises each day and enjoy the silence of being in your home without the intrusion of your family.
- If possible, walk one mile each day. Give to yourself before you give to anyone else.

Acknowledge your frustrations with the world.

There are countless social issues that demand our attention, all important and urgent.

- Ask yourself: What irks you personally? Homelessness? Failing education systems? The water crisis? Climate change?
- Try watching a few documentaries to see what issues you really care about.

Create a family practice of service.

First, call a family meeting. Then go around the table and let each member identify an issue that is troubling them, or something that is important to them. (See the previous assignment.)

Brainstorm together how that could translate to volunteering. For example, if someone at the table says they are worried that old people get lonely, perhaps the volunteer activity would be reading to senior citizens. Let every member of the family put their volunteer idea into the hat, and then every week (or month) pick out one idea to execute as a family. But don't throw out the other ideas! Make your way through the entire hat, and then have another family meeting to refill it with a new batch of ideas.

Here are some more ideas to get you started: When coming up with ways to volunteer, choose an activity that allows you to use your passions and talents, one that you may not get to use at your job. Consider reading to children at your local kindergarten or reading to senior citizens. Collect sanitary napkins for homeless youth. Build a book corner for youth in your hair salon or barbershop. Organize a tree-planting event in your neighborhood. Write letters to sanitation workers. Make cards for children in the ICU. Donate books to elementary schools. Teach English to second-language learners.

Start a giving jar. Volunteering through personal action is critical, but so is providing monetary support. Good deeds are not always enough, particularly for organizations that service girls. Though philanthropy is a multibillion-dollar industry, according to the Women's Philanthropy Institute only 1.6 percent of financial support goes to organizations that provide for women and girls. Teresa Younger of the Ms. Foundation for Women describes this lack of patronage in this way: "In most cases, usually women are running very efficient organizations and paying themselves and relying on the kindness of their communities to allow them to do the work that needs to be done." Therefore, in addition to volunteering, I encourage you and your girl to develop a practice of making financial contributions to organizations or issues of interest.

Financial analysts suggest that we donate at least 3 percent of our earnings. For girls who get monthly allowances, this may be feasible, and as a parent, you can choose to match their giving. For those who do not get allowance, you can help them develop monthly entrepreneurial activities where they set a financial goal and fundraise to support a cause they care about. Fundraising activities can be done through setting up a lemonade stand, organizing a walk, or even doing extra chores.

3

Cultivating Gratitude

The foundation of volunteerism lies in cultivating gratitude within ourselves and our children. Being grateful means we have the ability to recognize, respond, and connect to others' needs, and this connection to others is the key factor in being joyful and a change-maker. Therefore, being grateful is essential for change-making and is akin to joyfulness. Joy, gratitude, and change-making are inextricably linked. Joyful people are grateful and will express their gratitude through their relationships and actions.

The source of gratitude is a belief in reciprocity, specifically, upstream reciprocity—the idea that what we do to help others will meet their needs and create a positive experience for them so that they feel compelled to pay it forward. This is distinctly different from downstream reciprocity, which is primarily concerned with gaining reputation and status from giving.

Gratitude is not simply an accounting of the ways our material resources (such as property, clothing, and money) and social positioning are better than others. Gratitude is tied to reciprocity, which centers connection with self and with others. The heart of gratitude is connection: emotional and social.

Beth insisted that she understood what was being asked of her. She made it clear that she understood the principle of reciprocity, but there was little evidence to show that she was grateful for the experience. Her outlook seems dim. Indeed, scholars have found that being grateful leads to positive outcomes, including happiness, well-being, life satisfaction, and less envy compared to individuals with a lower disposition toward gratitude. At that time, such things did not seem true for Beth.

However, gratitude is characterized not just by emotions, but also by expressions of kindness that lead to improved interpersonal relationships and community connectedness. Though the positive psychology movement has promoted the idea that individuals who practice gratitude will "flourish" (living a life with positive emotion, engagement, good relationships, meaning, purpose, and accomplishment), gratitude is not singularly self-serving. Being grateful can enable us to better help others to improve community wellness and justice.

Scientific evaluations of gratitude have shown that adults are better able to conceptualize the idea than children. Preteens may be too young to fully understand the emotions of gratitude. Therefore, to develop a devotion to gratefulness, children need to witness multiple and ubiquitous examples of gratitude in practice. Witnessing such actions will impact their future behaviors. Adults, namely parents, must model gratitude so children can understand how it operates. Observing repeated high-quality interactions and ongoing acts of gratitude can create a culture of gratitude—similar to those discussed in our conversation on volunteerism. Therefore, children will adopt such behaviors, emotions, and gratitude expressions as they grow. Moreover, they are likely to practice such actions in their social networks.

Researchers have found that people who witness expressions of gratitude will see its positive impact and therefore be more willing to help others in the future. Now here you might want to be cautious, as some children may see giving as performative and engage in such actions simply for the praise. To guard against this, it is important that parents frame and explicitly articulate to children that the basis of gratitude is responding to the needs of others. We must divorce gratitude and volunteerism from reputation.

The effort, then, toward engendering gratitude among children is to model the behavior. As parents, we begin with the one-to-one exchanges that happen when we volunteer. Children must witness our behaviors so that they can experience what scholars call "emotion contagion." Our girls can become infected with these principles and practices by seeing how we are transformed by being grateful and how our actions transform others. Parents must explain that gratitude strengthens the quality of relationships. And that emotional expression of being grateful can have reverberating effects for the entire community. Gratitude conveys that a grateful person acknowledges another's good deeds. It also demonstrates that responding to people's needs is valuable. To engender gratitude is to develop helping behaviors.

Gratitude is the relationship currency we need to create social change; it encourages generosity and strengthens social bonds. In fact, gratitude strengthens social bonds beyond simple economic exchange. Such feelings of thankfulness matter for our well-being and propel us into action.

While we are talking about gratitude, I want to give a shout-out to the middle class. Because middle-class adults are ideally placed to raise change-making girls. Now, this book is for *all* parents and caregivers, but the fact is, when families are struggling just to put food on the table, or make sure the lights stay on so their children can do homework, their resources—inner and outer—are most often dedicated to getting by, day by day, and making sure their children have roofs over their heads. When their family's safety is compromised, or their health is challenged, or their children's education is undermined, they likely don't have the resources to create social change through their parenting practices. Moreover, low-income people, unfortunately, are not in the rooms where the systems that create and perpetuate social inequities are designed. Rather, they are grappling with systems generated by those with greater economic power.

Though middle-class families have the necessary resources, sadly they often don't recognize the opportunity to think in these terms. They're more focused on their own achievements and on making sure *their* kids get what they need to thrive. Seldom do they consider that they're in a position to bring about meaningful social change—and that they can do this *by thinking about how they raise their children.*

But who is the middle class, really? Under President Barack Obama, the U.S. Department of Commerce's Middle Class Task Force prepared a report worth quoting:

> Middle class families and those who wish to be middle class have certain common aspirations for themselves and their children. They strive for economic stability and therefore desire to own a home and to save for retirement. They want economic opportunities for their children and therefore want to provide them with a college education.

It is impossible not to notice that this definition of the middle class is rooted in external, consumerist measures—a home, a car, annual family vacations—as well as a preoccupation with economic security for oneself and one's offspring. These are the well-meaning but often shortsighted parents who I most want to reach. Middle-class adults—and their children—have the social, political, and economic currency to create systemic transformation. They are also in influential relationships with people who can be levers for large-scale social change. I want these caregivers to understand that by developing a sense of communal responsibility and a culture of gratitude within their families, they can help to effectively lift up disadvantaged families—and change the world.

If there is one thing I want to say to middle-class parents, it is this: You have been deploying your resources singularly for you and yours. Stop doing that. Parent your children with a larger vision.

ASSIGNMENT

Practice gratitude.

Gratitude isn't an emotion to be reserved for those moments when you get what you want, when your needs are satisfied. Having gratitude is also important in times of disappointment. The power of gratitude enhances your life and improves the lives of others.

Here are some simple, daily ways to begin a life of gratitude.

- Place an object somewhere in your house or workspace that will remind you to feel grateful each time that you look at it. It can be a little sign that says "Thank You" hanging in front of your desk. Such reminders make the values we have visible and known; reminders help us stay the course and be true to our values.
- At the end of each day, take a mindful moment to acknowledge:

  - What moved me today?
  - Who or what inspired me today?
  - What made me smile today?
  - What's the best thing that happened today?

- Sit down and write a letter to someone whose good deeds have made an impression on you. This can be a grandparent or a teacher or mentor from your past whose actions are inspirational. The letter doesn't have to be long, but make sure that you're specific about what the person did and how it affected you. Send the letter.

4

Teaching Her to Celebrate Herself

~~~~~~

The inwardly content are able to handle love. And that calls, first and foremost, for joy of self. *It is the by-product of whole-hearted Self celebration that brings inner peace.*

—*Dorothy Corkille Briggs*

Caregivers, as you teach your girl to honor and appreciate others, you must also teach your girl to honor and celebrate herself. The year I turned seven, this quotation by Dorothy Corkille Briggs, author of *Celebrate Yourself: Enhancing Your Own Self-Esteem*, became real to me. It was February 11, 1979. My grandmother and my whole family forgot my birthday. My grandmother's two-bedroom wooden house in the rural hills of Jamaica was home not just to me, but also to my three older brothers, two aunts, several cousins, and my grandmother's husband—thirteen people in all. And they all forgot my birthday.

I tried to convince myself it didn't matter. Instead, I fixated on my favorite wish: that my father would visit on my birthday. At that age, having my father in my life was a constant fantasy of mine, even though I had never met him. All I knew of him was that he had left Jamaica a few months after I was born to rejoin his wife in the United States—mine is a complex family narrative, I know. My brothers all knew their fathers. These men sometimes showed up on their birthdays; on those days my brothers went off with their fathers and returned with gifts in hand and stories of fun outings. For months I had prayed this would be the year my own father finally arrived on my doorstep with a birthday present. In my mind, I had been laying the groundwork for this to happen, being extra good, because my grandmother had told me that God grants wishes to those who are good. In the weeks leading up to my big day, I had easily been the best-behaved child in our village.

On the morning of my birthday, I stood on my grandmother's veranda surveying the hillside, waiting for my wish to be fulfilled. Imagine my excitement when I saw a truck weaving up the gravel road to our house. *It's my dad! It's my dad!* I screamed over and over inside my head. The truck pulled into the driveway, and a tall man emerged from behind the wheel. A man I loved. But it was not my dad. It was my Uncle Peter, my mother's brother. And he had remembered my birthday.

I jumped down off the veranda and ran to meet him, laughing as he swooped me into the air, singing his rendition of the happy birthday song. He set me back on my feet and handed me a box of Excelsior crackers and a bottle of Guinness. I am sure these items were not originally intended as gifts, but feeling the need to comfort me, he gave them to me. My grandmother and my Aunt Joyce rushed out of the house, gasping, "Lord, we forgot Janice's birthday!" My grandmother was especially shamefaced because, as she would later tell us, my mother had sent money from Canada, asking that I be given a cake and a new dress.

Uncle Peter noticed the tears building up in my eyes. He took my hand and walked with me to the top of the yard. "It's all right," he said as he comforted me. He pried the cap off the bottle of Guinness with his pocket knife and handed it to me. As I put the cold, fizzy liquid to my lips, he told me something that I would never forget. "Listen, you've got to learn to celebrate yourself, who you are *in here.*" He pointed to his heart. "If you do that, you won't need anyone else to do it for you."

Years later, as a teenager living in Massachusetts with my mother, her boyfriend, and some of my brothers, I needed to remember this lesson about celebrating myself. I used to watch *Diff'rent Strokes* on television, marveling at how Americans seemed to love birthday parties and assuming that now that I was living in America, I too would have big celebrations with friends and family. But in fact, my birthdays would continue to come and go without any hoopla.

It wasn't just birthdays that seemed to go unnoticed. In middle school, I was valedictorian, scoring in the top percentile of the Massachusetts examination to get into one of the top three magnet schools. I came in second in the science fair for my project on radon. I also won the IBM Excellence Award in social studies. Yet there were no special dinners or parties to celebrate.

Though my family may not have showered me with praise, I vividly recall feeling very proud of myself and my accomplishments. Child development research does not have much to say about self-praise. Therefore, little is known about what children do and think when adults ignore or overlook their achievements. Despite this oversight in the academic literature, there is some promising research evidence to show that what I did as a child, the act of feeling good about my individual success, was invaluable for bolstering my self-esteem, offsetting depression, and creating greater levels of internal happiness.

Without much prompting, as a kid I engaged in a lot of positive self-talk. I used, and still use, the ongoing dialogue in my head and a set of affirmations to boost my sense of self. I often repeated to myself the same phrase: "You can do this, Janice. You can do this."

I understood very early that people around me, especially my mother, never sought to hurt me. Their bad actions were not intentional, but rather circumstantial. My mother did not know she needed to praise me. As an economically struggling mother seeking to provide for four children, three of whom needed her attention more than I did, she was simply doing her best—in my eyes that best was not good enough, but I understood it as her best. Our mother worked between eighteen and twenty hours per day. She left at six o'clock in the morning, returning every two days for a few hours. During her time at home she made dinner for three days, organized our meals, took a short nap, left instructions of what to do, and then returned to work. She was a live-in home-health aide for the elderly. We had food and we had education, and I knew that we were lucky and more fortunate than other children. So when I didn't get the emotional support I needed, I relied heavily on myself. Affirmations were my psychological resource that helped me cope with ongoing threats to my sense of self.

The lack of familial support seemed to change on my sixteenth birthday. Fully expecting to be shot down, I asked my mom if I could have a Sweet Sixteen party. Now, my mother did not like us to have people over. I was never sure exactly why. The house was kept in good repair, but perhaps she was embarrassed by the fact that her four children shared a single bedroom. Or perhaps she wanted to shield people from the disagreeable personality of my stepfather. Maybe she just wanted peace and quiet. Yet to my surprise and shock she said yes to my party on the first ask, on the conditions that I hold it in the basement rather than the living room and keep the invitees to five friends, no more.

I was so elated by her yes that the conditions did not bother me. I already knew who I would invite. The morning before the party, my brothers and stepfather helped me clear a small area downstairs for dancing, and we set up a table for cake and food. For music, I decided to use my brother Andrew's boom box, on which I would rotate two custom-made cassette mixtapes of rap and reggae songs that he'd made for me.

On the night of my birthday, as each friend arrived, I answered the doorbell eagerly. I was beyond excited at the chance to create my perfect party. I knew we wouldn't have the freedom of teens in movies like *Weird Science* or *Sixteen Candles,* but I did think we would laugh and dance all night long. Unfortunately, the evening did not go as I'd planned.

My mom sequestered herself in her bedroom so as not to hear us, while my stepdad kept coming down to the basement, checking to make sure we were not disturbing his things. His Jamaican accent was so thick that none of my friends could understand anything he said, but there was no mistaking the annoyance in his tone. Every time he appeared, the energy in the room dampened, until we began waiting stiffly for his next visit. Less than an hour in, I resignedly asked my friends to leave. What was the point of having a party if you couldn't enjoy it? I was too frustrated to enjoy myself. From that misbegotten night until I graduated from high school, I never attempted to host another party at our house, nor did I invite anyone over for a visit.

Twelve years later, at age twenty-eight, it was resoundingly clear that I had strong feelings about my birthday. It was also the year that I met my dad for the first time. I worked in midtown Manhattan, living uptown in Harlem. Exhausted from a long day of work, I decided to forgo taking the two trains I would typically ride to commute home and took a cab instead—a life-changing decision, it turns out.

A few minutes after pulling away from the office, the cabdriver began talking to me. Irritated by his constant chatter, I asked glibly, "What island is that I hear in your voice?"

"Grenada," he said. "Why do you ask?"

"I am supposed to know a Jamaican cabdriver," I responded with snark in my voice.

"*Supposed?*" he asked, surprised.

"Yes, my mother once told me that my father is a cabdriver in New York."

"Really, what's his name?" the cabdriver asked.

"Amos Johnson," I said.

"Amos, I know him," he said, and I rolled my eyes at this unbelievable tale. New York City has eight million people and thirteen thousand yellow taxis. How could this random cabdriver know the one man I had waited to meet my whole life?

When we pulled up to my apartment in Harlem, the driver asked for my business card. "I am sure Amos would love to know his daughter."

Whatever, dude, you don't know him, I thought to myself. Still, I gave him my card, thinking nothing would come of it.

Much to my surprise, a few weeks later while en route to San Diego (my work took me to California each month), I got an early morning cell phone call from a man claiming to be Amos Johnson. Warily, I agreed to meet him when I returned to New York. Then I called my mother and told her. She was elated, almost as if she had been waiting as long as I had. I asked her for some identifying detail that only she and he would know, a way for me to make sure it was him. Then my mother blew apart my world by telling me that she had lied to me my whole life about why my dad was absent from my childhood. She had told him to leave. At the time of my conception and birth, she had known that he was married. And when he received word from his wife in America about a visa, she had encouraged him to leave because there were so few economic opportunities in Jamaica. I was shocked, but for the moment her dissembling took a back seat to the fact that I would finally meet this man.

Two weeks later in late December, I returned to New York City. Amos and I agreed to meet at Copeland's, a soul food restaurant on 145th Street, just walking distance from my apartment at 143rd and Convent Avenue. As I entered the restaurant, I saw a man standing in the doorway. He stood about six feet two inches tall and wore gabardine pants; they were slightly too short, though nicely pressed. His collared white shirt looked like it had been spray-starched; the edges looked stiff. He was clean-shaven and, by all accounts, an attractive older man in his late sixties. As I walked through the door he tried to hug me.

This ain't the Oprah show, man. I don't know you, were my inner thoughts. But to demonstrate civility, I simply smiled, stood back, and shook his hand. The waitstaff found us seats in a booth near the back.

Using the information that my mother gave me, I verified that he was indeed Amos Johnson from Port Maria, Jamaica. We then called my mother on the phone, and they laughed out loud. It all felt so surreal. It was him. I didn't quite have a good handle on my feelings.

I learned about his five other children. He explained why he had not come back to see me in Jamaica after leaving. He also attempted to offer an explanation for why he had been absent from my life for twenty-six years, though he knew where I was. (His sister, an aunt I did not know well, had maintained a good relationship with my mother and kept tabs on my whereabouts.)

We talked for hours, but try as I might, I could not feel warmly toward him. The explanations he offered for his failure to contact me were all shallow and inexcusable. Still, I remained optimistic and cordial because I presumed that after that day, now that I had met him, I would have plenty of chances to come to terms with my feelings. I was nursing my inner disdain and frustration but worked hard to keep my face neutral. I'm not sure if I was successful, but I did try.

At the end of the evening, he asked if he could pick me up and take me to work the following week. I agreed. Who would give up a free cab ride to work? Not me. The next week he arrived at seven o'clock and drove me to work. There was something cool and weird about the whole experience. We didn't talk about much; the drive seemed particularly short, and before I knew it, I was at Fortieth Street and Third Avenue and had to leave. He wished me a good day and I did the same. I wouldn't talk to him again for several days. I knew his birthday was December 29 (my mother always mentioned it), just a few days from our first meeting, so I called him on his birthday to wish him well.

A few days later, the New Year came. He called and asked to meet; I agreed. The visit was short. He came to my apartment, and I met him outside. We made small talk, and within ten minutes I was back inside. I saw him twice more after that—both seem so forgettable now. In anticipation of February, I reminded him that it was my birthday on the 11th. "I know that," he said emphatically. "I will talk to you then." I worked the whole day in full expectation of a call from him to say happy birthday. I even assumed he might ask to drive me home from work as he had done before. I took the train home and celebrated with my boyfriend. We had Jamaican food and watched a Kung Fu movie. Just as I had done twenty years earlier on that very same day, I kept my expectations, and later my feelings of utter disappointment and sadness, to myself. But my birthday came and went and no call came.

Amos called a week later. He apologized for missing my birthday. With both absolute clarity of mind and deep feelings of hurt, I said, "I do not need to know you or have you in my life. My life is full and good and happy. Take care. Do not call me again." I have not spoken to Amos Johnson since.

I like to think that my Uncle Peter would be proud of me. As he had told seven-year-old me, I was worthy of celebration. As an adult, celebrating me was not my father's responsibility; it was mine. I must honor me, and it is for that reason that I have taken my birthday festivities to new heights. Each year since then, I have held intimate gatherings with dear friends. These get-togethers begin with a formal announcement to my friends via phone call, text, email, or social media in the month leading up to my big day: My birthday is coming. My birthday is coming. Rather than expecting that others will remember, I cheerfully remind everyone of the date and its importance to me.

The year I turned thirty-six, I planned the grandest celebration yet. Over the course of one week I held birthday gatherings in six of the seven U.S. cities where I had lived, plus one more in Barbados. Starting from my home base in West Orange, New Jersey, I crisscrossed the country from New York to Boston to Philadelphia to Washington, D.C., then to Los Angeles, ending with a weeklong party on a beach in Barbados. All the celebrations were small and beautiful, spent with people who had always supported and loved me.

I enjoy celebrations because of their intimacy and the opportunity to connect with those you love and who love you back. Though I value my birthday, I also celebrate small moments and goals. When something good happens to me, I might rejoice by taking a walk while listening to music. I often host impromptu events for myself, my friends, and my family, usually for no reason at all other than the pleasure of being together. When my husband, Scott, received a promotion at work, I surprised him by having a few friends over, and each person spoke about how proud they were of him. If Marley achieves something that she has worked on—for example, when she completed gymnastics class—we hold a gathering for her at the house, serving her favorite apple-juice-pumpkin muffins to her closest aunties and friends.

Studies show that, whether big or small, celebrations matter because they offer opportunities to reflect and show gratitude. Enjoying big and small celebrations adds a little ceremony to life, and birthdays, in particular, matter because they signify your beginning and the joy of life. With our birth, we are given a chance to fulfill our unique purpose, and those moments are worthy of recognition. But it is the collection of thousands of small cheerful observances that builds the habit to celebrate, which in turn helps to hardwire these virtues and values into our children.

Though a child's environment can fuel motivation because it may offer praise, not all children will receive that recognition or be in supportive environments that salute them. Therefore, it is essential that all children have self-affirmations and pride in themselves to boost their self-esteem *and* improve their self-efficacy—that is, their capacity to create change outside of themselves. Celebrating and honoring themselves will put girls in an ideal position to feel good about themselves, conceptualize ideas, and feel capable of leading initiatives.

Feeling like you are a person of worth—having good self-esteem—is essential for all of us, but especially for girls. Having high self-esteem gives girls the confidence they need to be joyful, which in turn helps them feel powerful enough to want to change the world.

Very young girls often have a high valuation of themselves that declines over time. In our work at SuperCamp we find that elementary school–age girls have good self-esteem; they do not have difficulty identifying and naming the things they are good at and things they like about themselves. They are unabashed. Without shame and often with much pride, they quickly and easily respond to probing questions about themselves. "I am a really good speller." "I can run faster than everyone in my class." "I am really smart." "Every time I get a good grade I dance around my room." They enjoy and celebrate themselves consistently.

As girls move from elementary to middle school and further into puberty, their positive self-evaluations decline; their self-esteem decreases. They become more self-critical and more aware and cautious of the ways they are perceived. They are concerned about being seen as too self-congratulatory, so they wait for others to congratulate them. The internal power they had when they were young begins to wane as external evaluations begin to have more value. This process continues as they age; by the time they get to high school, girls have to be reminded that it is okay to feel good about their own skills and talents. Though the self-confidence of tween and early teen girls plunges, they continue to outperform boys academically. Consequently, many people mistake their success for confidence.

In an effort to ensure that girls do not lose that childlike confidence, we at GrassROOTS employ a family systems model premised on the idea that well-being and harmony begin with the self. We work with our girls so they are reminded to celebrate themselves before they celebrate others. This model demands, then, that individuals in families, primarily their caregivers, celebrate themselves—again serving as models for their children. (More about this in Part II.)

During community circle at camp, we ask each person, parent or girl, to say something they really like about themselves. When adults, particularly mothers, are able to name things they like about themselves, it gives girls permission to do the same. We also ask caregivers to name a way they celebrate themselves. Often, this exercise identifies a gap. Sure, some moms pamper themselves once a month with a spa date or shopping trip, but on average, most caregivers do very little to celebrate themselves. The revelation that they do not celebrate themselves often creates a somber mood during circle time, but this is where we find opportunities to teach our girls about the value of breaking the cycle and creating new opportunities for themselves.

In our one-to-ones with girls, we ask them to reflect on learning that some adults do not celebrate their achievements. Oftentimes girls find it sad that parents' lives don't seem very joyful. The absence of joy in parents provides the opening for girls to see value in being different from their parents and to become joy seekers.

We try to make it clear that celebration of self should be a daily part of their lives. They do not need to reserve a special day of the month or have money to honor who they are. Our goal is to get girls to the point where their daily self-talk involves saying something positive and affirming to themselves about themselves—even if their parents don't do it for them or for themselves.

Take the case of Lucy, a fun, charming little girl who I have known since she was four years old. Always sweet. Not known for her academic skills—a valued talent for her parents—she never received much acclaim. She has two older brothers; one was a top scholar and the other a top athlete in their schools. As the one and only girl in the family, without any recognizable and cherished skills, she struggled with feeling appreciated. Her low self-confidence was palpable. She made fun of herself openly and could always be found messing with her hair and pulling at her clothing.

During community circle, she was asked what she liked about herself. She responded, "I am nice." Nice is a nondescriptive adjective; the word offers very little substance. When probed to say what "nice" meant, she was stumped. It was clear to us that we would have to find ways to help her become more self-assured.

The task of getting girls to see themselves as valuable and feel good about who they are takes a lot of work. The heart of the struggle lies in helping them understand their value and distinguishing what others say or have said about them from their own thoughts and feelings about themselves. The one-on-one therapeutic care with the licensed therapist is a critical part of this work, but so is our consistent reinforcement of the principle of truth: Each person is worthy of celebration. We also work with girls to create their own affirmation in the form of an "I am . . ." statement. For Lucy and girls like her who faced a similar issue, we often had them repeat the phrase "I am proud of myself" followed by an action that they took. "I am proud of me for trying my best," "I am proud of me for pushing past my fear," or "I am proud of me for remembering to pack my bag." Insisting that they value a small accomplishment makes room for them to value other bigger things about themselves.

Our efforts at SuperCamp focus on helping girls understand and appreciate their unique genius. This demands that their care circle (close family, including siblings and parents) note the reward systems they have in place at home that diminish their children's self-esteem. In Claire Shipman, Katty Kay, and JillEllyn Riley's 2018 article "How Puberty Kills Girls' Confidence," they reference the academic research explaining how girls become dramatically less self-assured over time. The evidence shows that parents and teachers frequently encourage and reward girls' people-pleasing, perfectionistic behavior, without understanding the consequences. Often, this is because it just makes parents' and teachers' lives easier: In a busy household or noisy classroom, who doesn't want kids who color within the lines, follow directions, and don't cause problems? But perfectionism, of course, inhibits risk-taking, a willingness to fail, and valuable psychological growth.

Lucy's genius was more recognizable in her artistic than her academic talents. Because of the open and unstructured time at camp, we were able to observe how much she loved to dance. When she danced, her unbridled self and the joy inside of her was made manifest to the world. She came alive. Through lots of encouragement and hard work, we motivated her to showcase her talents at the final performance. Working closely with her mom and the dance instructor, Lucy choreographed her own dance. She practiced at home, which gave her mom an opportunity to see Lucy come alive. Rehearsals were hard. Though she often struggled, she pushed through. Over four weeks, she became more confident. You could see it in her smile. She was clearly feeling more capable because she was improving, and she was indeed feeling more confident. On more than one occasion, I observed her talking to herself during difficult times, repeating the phrase, "I can do it." And she did do it. She performed a breathtaking dance at the SuperCamp final performance.

Though the performance was good, I was still concerned about what she had learned from the experience. The work was not about the outward gratification or applause. It was about her self-development. Did she learn anything about herself? So I had to ask. Once she left the stage, I rushed over to her and asked, "How do you feel?" She was crying. She said that she felt good. "Great!" I responded. Then, filled with trepidation, I gingerly asked, "Are you proud of yourself?"

"I did it," she said. "I [long pause] did it." I was elated for the moment, but I was not certain that this lesson would stick with her. But one year later, her mom called me and asked for a tutor referral for Lucy. She had fallen behind in school and wanted to catch up with her peers. She approached her mom and asked if she could get additional help to get back on track. In the telling of the story, her mom said, "She felt like she could really do it if she set her mind to it." Lucy said she knew she had it inside her. The lesson to celebrate herself was sticking. She was seeing the value in self-praise. Celebration of yourself is about feeling worthy; it is often tied to feeling capable. In my experience, writers like Claire Shipman, Katty Kay, and JillEllyn Riley are right. "Confidence is an essential ingredient for turning thoughts into action, wishes into reality. Moreover, when deployed, confidence can perpetuate and multiply itself."

Phara's story shares the same underlying themes about celebrating oneself. Nine-year-old Phara is a precocious girl with lots of energy. But, like Lucy, she was not academically inspired; instead she was much more interested in people. When it came time to memorize and perform a poem, she struggled. She could not focus her attention on books or schoolwork. When we queried her about the source of her challenges, she responded defeatedly, saying, "I am not good at studying." Feeling deflated, she would stomp off during rehearsal of her poem.

Admittedly, I had a special affinity for Phara. She was a refugee from the 2010 earthquake in Haiti. She knew abandonment well. She had an accent and spoke mostly Haitian Creole and French. Though she clearly had lots of internal reserves, she did not quite know how to access them on her behalf. Her inner dialogue focused more on surviving than thriving. I was personally devoted to providing her with new words to say to herself. I decided to mentor her, spending a lot of time with her so I could understand the source of her struggles. I used the same exercise with her as I did with Lucy, asking Phara to tell me the things she said to herself when she had done something of which she was proud. "I don't do anything that I am proud of," she would glibly respond. This response startled me.

She could not take account of her wonderful attributes. She was the one who ran to aid girls when they needed help and looked out for younger girls, making them laugh when they seemed sad. She was always the first to clap for someone when they excelled at an activity. She was the first to help staff when we were bringing things in for delivery and among the first to help set up for lunch. She was the consummate cheerleader. It was important to me that she understand that these attributes are important; they didn't just make her "nice"—they made her wonderful, helpful, and kind.

Though it took several weeks and many conversations with me, the team, and the therapist, Phara eventually realized that the way she treated others was the way she needed to treat herself. Though she struggled with her own poem, she wanted to help the younger girls with theirs. So we made a deal. She could not help anyone until she had mastered her poem: "I, Too, Sing America" by Langston Hughes. To help her connect, I changed the last sentence in the poem to French so that she could better relate to Hughes's message. We agreed that she would do this poem because at the heart of the poem is Hughes's declaration that Black folks also belong in America. The speaker in the poem is declaring a sense of belonging and asserting their right to be seen. Immigrants, internal and external, often have to undergo this process of belonging to a new place. This was my story, and it was also Phara's. The poem ends with a celebration of self. For days, during her free time, Phara practiced. And on the sixth day, during community circle she asked to recite her poem to the group with the last line changed. She nervously made her way through the poem, and with confidence she uttered: *"Je suis l'Amérique"* as the last line. The words left her lips with such passion. She, too, was America.

Though she had been born on a different isle, it was clear in her words that she understood the intent and meaning of Hughes's words. The assertion of selfhood was evident on her face. The group of girls erupted in applause. However, their joy, though clearly meaningful, had less value than the sense of personal accomplishment on Phara's face. As with all things, we debriefed; she was infinitely proud of herself. She had met her goal. She had done it; she memorized the poem and felt powerful, so much so that she started to finally talk about Haiti. And best of all, she could now help the younger girls. She had something to offer them. She was an example of accomplishment.

ASSIGNMENTS

Help your girl develop a positive self-talk habit. Help her create an affirmation.

To get started with creating more positive self-talk, help your girl develop and choose affirming and motivational mantras she can use throughout the day and again at night. This could be a simple private declaration, such as "I am powerful," or the mantra "[Insert her name], you got this." At the end of each day, ask her to share with you something about herself that she is proud of. Routinize these small celebratory moments until she starts coming to you, screaming out: "Wanna hear what I did today? I am so proud of myself for . . ." The more she is able to see herself as the subject of her story, the more confident she will become. These moments are not about self-aggrandizement. The focus should be identifying and recognizing the power of her own agency and her ability to overcome real or imagined obstacles.

Create and surround your girl with positive mental images or visualizations of success.

The phrases and words we choose should be those that can propel us toward our goals. These mental images create visual pictures of ourselves doing exactly what we say we want to do, and they create imprints in our minds. Fundamentally, they tie our beliefs to our actions.

- Take a few minutes with your girl to visualize yourselves doing the things you want. Focus on the feelings you want to have at the end of an activity or experience. Let your thoughts linger on these images until the emotions become real for you. Practice these visualizations daily. They are useful in your fitness program, for your courageous conversations, on a work project, etc.
- Use these visualization exercises to create a yearly vision board. A vision board is an excellent way to help you and your girl identify, define, and clarify what you really want in your lives. Focus on goals and empower your girl to create the life she imagines through the identification of goals.
- As a reminder, the purpose of these boards is to help you and your girl generate a new plan, develop different outlooks, and formulate alternatives.

For your girl's next birthday, ask her what she wants to do.

What may be celebratory to parents may not have value for their daughters. Plan your girl's party together, the refreshments, party favors, guest list, theme—all of it. Make the process as collaborative as possible. Begin this practice as early as five years old, and over time, share with her your budget so that she is aware of the parameters. Develop an annual tradition of creating this special day together so that, no matter what, she feels special about her birthday. It is also important that she understands that her birth-*day* and the celebration of her birth may not happen on the same day. Celebrations of her life can happen on the weekend of her birthday, the week before, or the week after. The only way she will understand this nuance is if you explicitly explain it to her. So begin now; start talking with her.

Note: She will learn how to celebrate herself if you provide her with an example. For your next birthday, plan a party with a purpose. Birthdays will come every year, like it or not. But you can decide what your birthday can mean to you, and how it should be celebrated.

In 2011, I celebrated my birthday by planting the seeds for GrassROOTS Community Foundation. Having fully celebrated myself for so many years, I now wanted to share the bounty. Months before the big day, I had decided that, for my birthday, I would host an event to raise funds to support girls who currently live in poverty. Eighteen friends across seven states and I organized a party that would have a social justice purpose. I called on an old friend and Philadelphia neighbor, Tariq "Black Thought" Trotter from the band The Roots and a regular on *The Tonight Show Starring Jimmy Fallon,* and he agreed to headline the event. (Tariq had lived upstairs from me while I was a graduate student at Temple University.) Though I had no money to pay him, he nonetheless agreed to travel from New York City to the venue in Philadelphia to perform. With the help of word of mouth, fifty dollars' worth of promotional flyers, and lots of fundraising pledges, we held the party on a rainy Friday night in West Philadelphia. People showed up from all across the United States. We charged $20 as the entrance fee, and by the end of the night had raised a total of $28,000. And, just as my friends and I had promised, we gave it all away. The celebration of my life helped me discover my passion for giving. In the book *We Gave Away a Fortune,*

Christopher Mogil maintains that, when we give, we gain far more than we lose. This assessment is so absolutely true for me. We used the funds raised by my birthday party to support an after-school program for girls in Philadelphia and to start the GrassROOTS Community Foundation.

Part II

~~~~

Who Are You?

5

What Is Your Story?

$\sim\sim\sim\sim\sim\sim\sim\sim\sim\sim$

As you might have figured out by now, a crucial aspect of this book—and of the work we do with families at GrassROOTS—relies on us recognizing and modeling the characteristics we want our daughters to inherit. Such a high standard demands that we infuse a devotion to social justice and desire for joy into our parental practices so our girls can be inspired not just by our words, but also by our actions. Because, as W.E.B. Du Bois observed, "Children learn more from what you are than what you teach." We aren't perfect—as parents, we are human and we come with our own history of hurts—but it's important to look in the mirror ourselves, before we turn to parenting our girls. So if there is something we don't like or don't recognize, we have to do the work on it.

For me, this meant reconciling my definitions of parenthood as I had learned them from my family, and also learning how to value myself as part of that equation, fractured though it might be. This lesson was driven home to me when I was pregnant with Marley.

I spent the whole nine months of my pregnancy assuming that when it was time for me to give birth, my mother, Monica, would travel to Philadelphia from Boston to help her only daughter learn the ropes of motherhood. It never occurred to me that she wouldn't share my plan.

But as nine months pushed toward ten—because as every woman who ever carried to term will tell you, pregnancy is ten months long—my mother still hadn't made any arrangements. Finally, I called her.

"Mommy, when are you coming?"

"Why would I?" she replied matter-of-factly. "I did this four times on my own. You don't need me. You'll be fine."

I was floored. I shouldn't have been.

The year I turned two, my mother secured a visa to work as a live-in nanny in Canada, and she left my three older brothers and me with our grandmother to move overseas and raise another family's children. Painful as it was for her, the tradeoff was better pay than she would ever see in Jamaica, and the promise of a better life for us. But while she sent money and shipped barrels of clothes and school supplies home to us every year, I had no memory of her before I was nine years old. Nor did I know my father, who had migrated to America when I was still a baby.

You see, my mother had always been a maverick. Uncommonly beautiful, she carried herself regally, even as a child—as I was told by my grandmother and aunts. Unfortunately, some of the men in our village seemed to believe she was open and available for their sexual advances. My mother tried to tell her own mother what was happening, but my grandmother didn't believe her. So, at age twelve, my mother packed her few things and moved to the larger neighboring town of Port Maria, where she rented a room and eventually got a job at the brassiere factory. From that day on, she relied on no one but herself for financial support. She bore each of her children by a different man, but chose to marry none of them. Whatever others might have thought of her choices, she neither explained nor apologized. Today she owns an apartment building in Boston, the city to which she eventually migrated, and where she would finally reunite with all four of her children.

But even without my mother, I grew up in a household of women. In addition to me and my brothers, my grandmother housed four cousins, a great-aunt suffering from dementia, another aunt, and my grandmother's husband. It was a loving environment, yet all too often I felt like an abandoned child in their midst, disconnected from any parent, unlike my brothers, who received regular visits from each of their fathers. This sense of isolation would not lift until my mother returned.

I can still recall the afternoon I met my mother for what felt like the first time. I was nine years old. My aunt dressed my three brothers and me in our Sunday best, and we traveled by bus to the airport in Jamaica's capital city of Kingston. I was quivering with anticipation. As passengers began to stream out of customs, I surveyed them with a knitted brow. There was no way to know exactly which person was my mother. The only picture I'd ever seen of her was a blurry black-and-white photo that hung in the living room of my grandmother's house. Then my aunt said, "Go to your mother. She's the one in the red dress." Excited, I ran to the first woman I saw wearing a red dress, but she was a stranger. My mother stood a few feet away, devastated. She has never forgotten, and perhaps never forgiven, my innocent mistake.

But that wasn't the reason she was now refusing to come and help me care for my new baby. My mother wasn't sentimental, nor did she ever do anything simply because it was expected of her. She always did exactly as she pleased, and it didn't please her to come to Philadelphia and play the role of grandmother. Still, I was hurt by her choice and carried that pain with me for a long time.

The feeling my mother's decision evoked in me was not new, but I had been under the illusion that I had moved beyond such emotions. Instead, I was overwhelmed anew by a pain that was too familiar—the loss, the abandonment, it all came flooding back. It was as Nobel Prize–winning author Toni Morrison described in the documentary of her life, *The Pieces I Am:* "The darkest parts of myself, that I thought I had left behind, came creeping back in."

My grandmother, on the other hand, would always find a quiet time to sit and talk to just me, even though there were thirteen of us living under her roof. It was her way of checking in. She would sometimes ask me to walk next to her, whether we were on our way to the market or to church. My grandmother walked slowly and told great stories. And she would ask me *questions.* To this day, being asked questions is still one of the ways that I feel most heard and appreciated. Questions suggest that you are interested in what I am thinking.

I still remember my grandmother's Bible—it was well-worn, heavily annotated, and underlined, with old tattered pictures and scraps of folded paper tucked between the pages. On the nights that she felt tired before going to bed, she would ask me to read to her from it. This was another way that my grandmother made me feel seen, even in a household of several children. Despite her efforts, I was still always wanting, hungry for love and aching for my mother. Sure, I wanted that grandmotherly love, but most important I wanted to be parented—not grandparented.

So, at thirty-three years old, far from being a child myself, I was due to give birth and finally beginning to understand that I would have to parent myself. Just like the native root of the word *parent*—the Latin *parere,* which means "to give birth to, bring into being, produce"—that phone call reminded me that I would have to give birth to the self I wanted to be.

Fortunately, I had some emotional resources at my avail. As I contemplated my situation, I was reminded of a scripture from 1 Corinthians, chapter 13, that my grandmother had recited to me time and time again:

> When I was a child, I spoke as a child, I understood as a child, I thought as a child; but when I became a [wo]man, I put away childish things. For now we see in a mirror, dimly, but then face to face. Now I know in part, but then I shall know just as I also am known. And now abide faith, hope, love, these three; but the greatest of these is love.

I was now an adult and was going to have to put away childish things and feelings. With this in mind, I actively sought help to deal with the pain of abandonment that had been buried so deeply inside of me. I began talking openly about my feelings of insecurity at becoming a mother. I folded myself up in the arms of all the clinical social workers I knew, and I cried on the shoulders of my husband and my dearest friend, Mary. The tears flowed frequently and without warning—and at times they seemed never-ending. But they were necessary. I had to unburden myself to make space for this child to come into the world. Parenting yourself is an ongoing process and is something I still work on, even as I raise Marley.

6

Learn Your ACEs

~~~~~~

There are bad childhoods and there are *bad childhoods.* And it's not a contest. But here's what we know: Scholars have explored at length the relationship between parental practices and child development. Painful life events such as abandonment are described as Adverse Childhood Experiences, or ACEs. Experts suggest that ACEs include events during childhood that range from slightly severe to extreme. These events are typically chronic, and they happen in the context of the child's family or social environment, causing harm or distress. Typically, ACEs occur prior to age eighteen, but they can also wreak havoc with our emotional development as late as age twenty-nine. ACEs can include growing up in a household or environment where there is recurrent physical abuse, recurrent emotional abuse, sexual abuse, emotional or physical neglect; living with an alcoholic or drug abuser, an incarcerated household member, or someone who is chronically depressed, suicidal, institutionalized, or mentally ill; having a mother, father, or guardian who is treated violently; or losing a parent to separation, divorce, or some other reason.

According to Kaiser Permanente San Diego and the Centers for Disease Control and Prevention, 67 percent of the U.S. population has experienced at least one ACE, and more than 12 percent of us have had four or more adverse experiences during our developmental years.

Luckily, researchers have also found that it is possible to put in place protective factors that can limit and/or mediate the impact of these adverse encounters. Clinical psychologist Dr. Sandra Prince-Embury, author of the Resiliency Scales for Children and Adolescents, explains that "external supports including positive relationships, supportive family members, and mentors, can buffer the effects of adverse situations." Indeed, a chorus of academic studies on risk and resilience demonstrates that we can create environments that allow individuals who have experienced adversity to ultimately find success.

I have never been ashamed of my own harsh childhood experiences, but that doesn't mean I've always been able to process them or even fully come to terms with the way they have shaped me. For a long time, my ACEs lay dormant deep inside of me. So while I could easily recite my story of walking miles to school, growing up without electricity, having no indoor plumbing, and not knowing my mom or dad, rarely was I able to express or show how I *felt* about these lived experiences.

Study after study on these matters has shown that for children like me who are exposed to prolonged chronic stress, the road forward demands that we recognize the pain, extract the good from it, forgive those who harmed us, and be grateful for having survived. Christopher Peterson and Martin Seligman in their book *Character Strengths and Virtues* describe forgiveness as a trait of temperance and gratitude as a trait of transcendence. This restraint and state of grace builds resiliency.

Luckily, by the time I spoke to my mother over the phone, I had built connections with people who pushed me to describe and engage my feelings, who insisted that I mourn and unpack, think through and recover. I had seen a therapist while in college and intentionally sought ways to better understand myself. I had begun the work of attending to my emotional pain. I had put in place what social worker Corrinne Minnard calls the "building blocks" of resiliency. So when I hung up the phone, I did so knowing that, despite the pain I was experiencing, with enough protective factors, the problems from the childhood adversity I faced could be interrupted. I could learn to parent myself.

Eventually I came to a place where I could see many of my child-hood experiences and my relationship with my mother—despite their challenges—as resources rather than as burdens. Getting to a place where I could admit the resentment and hurt I felt as a result of that call with my mother was hard, mindful work. But I had de-veloped a set of coping mechanisms that helped me combat the ad-verse effects of the socioeconomic and emotional environment in which I was born. Researchers suggest that there are protective and foundational resources that contribute to building resilience. One of these resources, they argue, is gratitude. In short, the grateful person tends to be more resilient in the face of life's hardships.

My journey toward resilience and gratitude that would lead me to feel self-efficacious began when I was thirteen years old with one of the first people to invest in me: my history teacher at Woodrow Wilson Middle School in Dorchester, Massachusetts. He helped me enroll in after-school math and science classes at a local college and urged my mother to sign me up for the state examination for one of the three top magnet schools in Boston at the time. After I had passed the exam and was admitted to Boston Latin Academy (BLA), he suggested I take Latin classes during the summer before I en-rolled so that I would be ahead when the school year began.

At BLA, I found kids like me, immigrants and U.S. natives who had similar life histories. I also found romantic and platonic love that would contribute to my healing. I made friends so close that regardless of race, ethnicity, or socioeconomic circumstance, they felt like my sisters and brothers. Additionally, with the help of teachers and guidance counselors, I found my voice and developed my love for learning and oration. Though I did not know it at the time, multiple scientific studies (for example, the U.K.'s Foresight Mental Capital and Wellbeing Project) remind us that social rela-tionships are critical for promoting well-being and for acting as a buffer against mental illnesses. High school also gave me the chance to see other kinds of families and witness up close other forms of childhood pain. Having people invest their faith in me and broad-ening my horizons helped me understand that I was not alone, and I began to see myself more clearly.

It was also around this time that I met one of the many mentors who would guide me and help me understand the deep value and benefit of mentorship. While a sophomore in high school, I worked in the mailroom of a Boston law firm. On my first day, a very tall, skinny white man named Robert showed me the ropes. I liked him right off the bat. His hair was often in some disrepair but not enough to make him disheveled; his appearance sent the message that he was not invested in looks. His energy was light, like Bill from *Bill and Ted's Excellent Adventure*. A self-professed libertarian and misanthrope from Kingston, Massachusetts, he worked in the mailroom, but it was clear in the books by his computer and the way he spoke that he didn't *belong* in the mailroom. I would later learn that he had scored an almost perfect score on his SATs and attended Cornell as an engineering major, but had dropped out to pursue his life.

Despite the fact that I was Jamaican born and raised, generally synonymous with being eminently practical and sensible, I understood his decision. His reasons were unclear to me at the time, but given his personality, it felt right: He loved learning but did not like the rules much. Little did I know I would later follow in his footsteps.

Robert and I became fast friends. I was fourteen and he was twenty-two. Though he was young, he seemed both older and wiser than his years, yet deeply inexperienced at life. He had lived in only three places: Massachusetts, Ithaca, and California. I had lived in the same number of places but under significantly more varied circumstances, which made me feel more knowledgeable about the world, particularly about the lived experiences of people. After all, in three years I had moved three times, lived in two countries, and had gone from being Jamaican to being Black in America. Neither he nor I understood how our racial differences affected the way people responded to us in public; at the time this reality seemed unimportant to our friendship and love.

For three decades Robert was my teacher, my anchor, my friend, and my family. He taught me the importance of asking questions. He made me read *Time* magazine each week, including the column by George Will. As I'd done with my grandmother, we walked and talked together. After work, we strolled to Mrs. Field's cookie store in downtown Boston for ice cream and milk. En route, he would quiz me about what I had read the night before. Once we arrived, we sat for hours discussing the main themes of George Will's column. With each discussion I had to offer a critique and ask at least one question. I didn't realize he was sharpening my analytical skills.

Robert took great care to ensure that I became a good reader. He understood the value of literacy, something that would become a key foundation in my life's work and parenting practice. He was a ferocious reader. He wrote a synopsis of each book he read on a flashcard and kept these summaries in the books themselves. Unlike him, I grew up in households without books. Other than the Bible, I had read no other book at home before coming to the United States. In Boston, there were still very few books in our living room, including only three volumes of the encyclopedia, covering the letters J, K, and Q. My stepfather kept them under close watch because they were there mostly for show, to signal status, not for use. (Consequently, all my reports for school demanded that I find something from the J, K, or Q encyclopedia, as my school did not have a library.)

I worked with Robert for two years, and by the time I was ready to apply to college, he was there to help. Robert helped me write my college essay and reviewed all my schoolwork. But beyond help with my academic progress, he made me feel valued. When my family seemed to forget I was there, Robert did not. His friendship and love helped me soar academically and personally.

The literature on ACEs discusses mentors like Robert. The supportive environments they create can mitigate many of our adverse childhood experiences. Scholars agree that the more protective factors a child who is exposed to adverse encounters has, the more the overall impact of those ACEs is neutralized, thereby providing a springboard for success in school and in life. When people ask me, "How are you able to be so joyful?" the answer is clear to me. I was fortunate to have social spaces that were actively created for and around me, which counteracted some of the trauma of my family circumstances. These settings made it possible for me to be resilient. Becoming resilient allowed me to be the architect of my own liberty.

For me, the strength that I have to live a joyful life as a parent comes from a few key things: allowing my past experiences to serve as teachers, practicing gratitude, and prioritizing my passions such that my life has meaning and purpose. I hope to engender or enhance this type of resilience among caregivers so that they can move beyond their own childhood issues to raise liberated girls.

The tricky thing with ACEs is that some of us who have lived through them put on a pretty great show of being "just fine." We are busy, we are successful, we earn good money. We have the external pillars of a full life. But even so, take a look at the inside. Here I want to tell you about my friend Lisa.

I first met this high-achieving mom when she brought her daughter Amina to Marley's fifth birthday party. Instead of just dropping off Amina, Lisa stayed. It wasn't clear if she was staying to keep an eye on things, to socialize, or just to hover. Nonetheless, we started chatting and I learned she was divorced and living in the same West Orange, New Jersey, suburban community that my family had moved to three years before. Our daughters were in kindergarten together. By day, Lisa worked as a marketing associate with a big pharma company, making six figures. By night, she was an overwhelmed mom rushing to pick up her daughter Amina from afterschool care, hoping to spend some quality time with her between dinner and bedtime.

I was immediately drawn to Lisa, with her big smile and lively personality. But the more time I spent with her, the more I realized that she was sad down deep. I couldn't understand her unhappiness. Highly educated, with an MBA from Duke, she seemed financially comfortable and had a close family network. Yet, she felt disempowered and lonely. She didn't feel connected to other moms since her busy schedule left her with little downtime to have small talk during school pickups and dropoffs or at weekend sporting events, and Lisa herself never exercised—she insisted she didn't have time. She had no idea who the members of her local government were; she barely knew the names of the parents around her, and she had established no intimate relationships with her daughter's teachers. Life simply happened to her. She seemed to believe she had no agency in how her life unfolded.

As we became closer, Lisa shared a litany of childhood disappointments. Despite having an active stepdad, having an absent father resulted in her lack of confidence. She grew up in an environment in which skinny, dark-skinned girls were not considered beautiful. She had also suffered her share of adult pain, including infidelity and an emotionally devastating divorce. She was disengaged from her passions and struggled to see her own worth. But while Lisa's lack of connection puzzled me, I found myself more concerned about her daughter.

Like her mom, Amina appeared outwardly animated. She laughed a lot and seemed much more easygoing than my own daughter, who expressed her preferences and dissatisfactions emphatically. Yet in quiet moments I could see Amina's sadness. Despite her mother's financial security, Amina wore unflattering hairstyles, and her clothes were often too big for her small frame. Desperate to be liked, she chose friends at school who were popular but not very nice to her. When asked a question, no matter how benign, she would respond in a high-pitched, defensive tone. Her answers lacked depth and almost always seemed unconvincing. She would often give the response she thought the other person wanted to hear. She was a consummate people pleaser; it was as if she believed her own truths and desires were inadequate.

Marley and Amina's friendship meant spending more time with Lisa, and over time we developed a close friendship. Any help she received from me in cultivating her joy occurred because of our relationship; it was not orchestrated. Spending time together and talking led to me asking her two simple questions: What makes you happy? What are you passionate about?

It was a weekday afternoon at Lisa's house, and we were hanging out. I had just shared with her that I wanted to start GrassROOTS. She cheered me on enthusiastically. "Good for you," she said. I told her I had been thinking about it for a while, and given my particular talents I had just decided that I was going to do it. I wanted to do work that brought me real joy. I needed to keep my day job, but I needed more.

"You can do that, but I can't," Lisa said, frowning. I asked why not. In my estimation, she was in a better position than I was to do what I was envisioning. She had more resources, more targeted training, and more support. She lived in close proximity to her family. I, on the other hand, had no family in New Jersey. She had some savings and a higher salary. I had a paltry salary and little to no savings. As a professor, I always had work at home (e.g., grading papers, creating syllabi, responding to students and faculty), and the only folks I knew in New Jersey were other parents at my child's school, her teachers, and some folks at the gym. Most important, I had only fifty dollars to contribute to the start-up of this big idea.

Ironically, while Lisa saw my passions as a bundle of resources, I saw her economic security as a better set of assets.

I became intensely curious about why she thought she couldn't do what she wished. Why did she feel unable to do what would make her internally happy? So I probed her for an explanation, only to find that she didn't know anymore what made her happy. "I haven't thought about that kind of stuff for a while," she said. Her response utterly shocked me. It sounds so ridiculous to say now, but bolstering my internal happiness has been my primary focus for most of my life. I had little to no occupational ambitions. But here I was with a person who was just the opposite. I was intrigued.

"So does your job fulfill you?" I pressed. I love questions.

Lisa responded with an emphatic no and walked away from me. She *walked away from me*! She admitted that she had not given much thought to what made her really happy since she was focused solely on survival and helping her daughter have a better financial life than she did. As a first-generation immigrant, she believed that nurturing the ideas of her own joyfulness and passions was a distraction; her focus had to be on providing the best educational and financial foundation for her child. She thought her passions could wait till her retirement. Therefore, she had focused on succeeding professionally and economically—something clearly tangible and realistic. At that moment I realized that I had one resource that Lisa was lacking: I still had hope—hope that achieving joy was possible in the now. The conversation was distressing for both of us. I became invasively curious about why Lisa had not thought about her own dreams, and she became irritated by my foolish idealism.

Over the years, Lisa and I have had some intense and tough exchanges about passions and joy. She maintained that the way I thought about and constructed the world was idyllic. I thought the way she constructed the world was too utilitarian. These divergent perspectives led to real moments of tension. I would often ask Lisa, "How can you just get up and work all day and then come home only to do it again?" Angrily, she would respond: "I have to. I am a single mom. If I don't do that, then who will?" My inquiries into how she had organized her life often came back to two recurring themes: time and support. She felt deeply that because I was married I was better positioned than she was. Also, she felt that as a professor I had more time than she did. In her estimation, these two distinguishing features meant I was better positioned than she to have a joyful life.

By my account, she had discounted a few key details. She had a sister, mother, and stepfather nearby who could and would have assisted her, if only she had asked. Her income was two times mine, and she lived in a housing complex that had a gym and pool. Furthermore, she knew New Jersey well, having lived there for years, and had a network of friends and colleagues who all were accessible to her. She saw my grass as greener than hers and had not explored how to use her resources to benefit her life. When I pointed out these differences, she would brush me off by saying, "They are too busy to help." I responded, "Have you ever asked them?" It was clear that she had not. It would take almost a year of conversation before she decided that she would hire a nanny because she still refused to ask her family for support. But that did not end our constant disagreements about these issues. She still insisted that the joy and passion that I had for life was unachievable for her. She also scoffed at the idea that life itself needed joy and passion. Like so many, she thought those things were reserved for people who were independently wealthy or idealists or those without children.

She was a pragmatist charged with doing practical things and in my eyes, none of these things were fun at all. To quote her, "Not everything needs to be fun, Janice." "Why not, Lisa?" I would shriek in despair. " 'Cause life is not fun, Janice," was her repeated retort. These comments revealed our fundamental philosophical disagreement. For her, adulthood, even life itself, was a drudgery that you go through until you acquire enough wealth to enjoy life. And parenting was a sacrifice and a decision to grind and toil in order to give children a better chance. She was raising her girl to work hard rather than play hard so she could one day garner a six-figure salary.

Her own mom had done the same thing—she was on a path of repeating history. Her mom, Mrs. Barnett, was a registered nurse who had moved to New York City for a better life for her children. Like Lisa, she was a single mom of daughters. In the early 1990s, she had been recruited in the middle of a nursing shortage. She worked overtime to ensure Lisa and her sister never had to take out student loans. In her mind, if her girls earned advanced degrees, they would be free. She used her vacations to visit her family in Jamaica where she spent the few weeks working on family projects. Over the years, Mrs. Barnett, too, had lost track of her passions, pouring countless hours into providing a better life for her children and providing for her family back home in Jamaica.

To Lisa, I was a strange bird. Here I was, Jamaican as well but acting like a flower child. Sure, I was raising a smart daughter, but Lisa was convinced that my daughter, like me, would never have a lot of money—joyfulness instead of wealth. To Lisa, joyfulness obstructed wealth acquisition.

We were often at an impasse about these ideas. But there were moments of agreement—that fun mattered for children's well-being. One of those moments came when she observed me teaching kids, her daughter included, how to do mathematics. She asked me to pick Amina up from school because she was running late; however, she was not as late as originally expected. She arrived in the middle of one of my sessions with the kids. We were doing math problems using props and songs. The kids were all engaged, and even those who seemed to struggle with math understood the concept. Her daughter loved math, so she was excited to participate. We were learning together in a way that differed from the strategies Lisa had been using at home.

By her own report, their typical home-learning experience involved her and Amina at a dinner table with flashcards and worksheets, working math problems. The emphasis was on getting the right answers. Exploration and learning from errors were met with yelling and frustration.

I couldn't fathom that she thought this was a good strategy, but she did, and she would fuss at me when I laughed at how ridiculous it was to teach a child this way. She explained to me that that was the way she and I had been taught. She was correct. Whether in Jamaica or the United States, learning through memorization was indeed the dominant educational style—and it worked for us. Both of us were top academic achievers. But our children *are not us*. They are Americans. We are more educated than our parents; we were supposed to know more than they did at our age and we had more money and resources than they did. So it seemed to me that we could not have expected to teach our children the way we were taught. The logic was just so dumb to me. But not to Lisa. She, like so many, assumed that because her parents' parenting strategy worked for her—she was a highly successful businesswoman with two degrees—then the same style would work for her daughter, Amina.

This inane logic—at least that's how I found it—applied to her view of joyfulness and passion. Lisa was living a life without passion and joy. By her own report, she expected those things would come in retirement once her daughter had gotten older and all her major obligations were complete. However, she expected Amina to be internally peaceful now because she had provided her with all the economic securities she believed Amina needed. On this latter point, I was not kind or gentle in my objection. I knew her daughter well, and the little girl was deeply insecure and, in my estimation, unhappy. I argued that her unhappiness was really a reflection of her mother's own unhappiness. Well, as you might imagine, conversations about this topic did not go well. Lisa was pissed. I assumed she was, but in truth I did not care. For me, it was intolerable that she wanted her child to be happy but was unwilling to provide her with an example. How would or could a child know what to do if you don't give them examples? The expectations for the little girl were unreasonable.

My blatant anger about Lisa's behavior started to show up in our exchanges. And it also revealed for me a passion point. I was irritated that caregivers like Lisa and so many others had framed their parenting around the "do as I say, not as I do" model. They wanted their children to be joyful, active learners who cared about the world, but the parents were not those things. The pressure on the kids was inordinate and unfair.

Lisa's metamorphosis took time, as did my ability to understand how she was feeling. Her initial resistance crumbled when my engagement with her daughter shifted from sporadic after-school pickups to five days per week and eight hours per day for five weeks each summer during our SuperCamp intensive. Amina was among the original five girls who attended SuperCamp, and she has attended every summer for nearly a decade. The first two years of leadership training gave Lisa concrete evidence why joy mattered in parenting. This understanding came about through many tense and tear-filled exchanges. She consistently had to hear my badgering voice as I encouraged her to read articles by social scientists who described in depth the risk factors for girls of single mothers like Lisa. I insisted that she meet with the team psychologist who evaluated Amina and saw some causes for concern. Primarily, the therapist was concerned that Amina was not developing a strong self-esteem; she was relying on others to define who she was. She was also willing to fabricate information to gain the attention and friendship of others (see Appendix B).

Luckily, Lisa is an oppositional learner, meaning she is committed to proving others, namely me, wrong. She is also willing to read and study to better understand information. She was determined to show us that she was a great mom and that Amina was fine. In an effort to be a great mom, she was hyperdiligent about all the assignments we gave the girls and their caregivers. As a way to ensure that the girls and the families follow the four core principles of Maat, we asked that families do a series of daily exercises. Each one was geared to ensuring that parents talk with and to their children. They had to ask them questions about their beliefs and friendships. Parents also had to share what they learn and know about themselves with their children. These assignments revealed that many of Lisa's assumptions about who her child was conflicted with the reality of what the GrassROOTS team observed. Specifically, Lisa had assumed Amina loved the way she looked and that she was self-confident. When they had to complete the mirror exercise (see Chapter 1), she discovered that Amina did not like her face and wished to look differently. Though learning these things was painful, Lisa stayed the course. She approached each assignment with skepticism as well as a desire to learn more; she diligently followed the SuperCamp curriculum. With each assignment she saw dividends in Amina's well-being. Amina was becoming happier and more honest about her feelings. They were talking more and learning to better understand each other. The change in Amina elicited a change in Lisa. It was clear that when joy was no longer just a concept and became operationalized into day-to-day actions, Lisa became a believer.

Watching Amina grow made her ask herself the question that I had asked her several years prior, "What are you passionate about?" She told of her desire to see the world and to travel, to which I responded, "Why not travel?" In true Lisa fashion, she said, "I can't; I am a single mom." "Oh, okay, Lisa," I would respond glibly. She found my response rude, and it was rude, but I was exhausted from her glass-half-empty outlook. Amina overheard one of our conversations and proposed that she stay with her grandma while her mom traveled. *What a brilliant no-brainer,* I thought sarcastically. Lisa's mom, who by then had retired, leapt at the chance to spend more time with her grandbaby. She came to New Jersey while Lisa traveled. Despite her reservations, Lisa took her first trip in 2014, and Amina survived. Soon she discovered that working and traveling were not at odds. Since 2014, she has traveled to India, London, and many U.S. states without Amina. She has also shared her love of travel with Amina by taking her to Peru, Puerto Rico, Dominican Republic, Paris, and Ghana.

Today, Lisa and Amina are thriving. Amina has discovered her passion for theater and found a social issue of significance to her. She serves as GrassROOTS' international youth ambassador, helping to end period poverty by providing sanitary items for girls in Jamaica and Ghana. Lisa, who has adopted the moniker #globetrotter, is a vice president of marketing at a technology company. She is often stopped in the street, mistaken for the actress Danai Gurira. She has discovered her passion for addressing gender bias and pipeline-related issues in the world of business. Best of all, the mother-daughter team is now quite impressive. The journey to these emotionally healed selves was not easy. It was fraught with antagonism toward me and frustration with themselves and each other.

Watching Lisa grow taught me so much about what I was asking of parents and what was possible. It has helped me grow more empathetic to the work it takes to parent like it matters. It also gave me more insight into what is possible if we stay the course.

ASSIGNMENT

Allow past experiences to be your teachers.

Too often when bad things happen to us we find ourselves wallowing in self-pity. We may even inflict the pain we've endured on others. We take the "hurt people hurt people" approach, assuming that the intergenerational cycle of pain is unchanging. Some of us may swallow that pain, believing we are not worthy of having good things. I challenge you to consider an alternative response—find the gold in your challenges. In your journal, write down the answers to these questions:

- What insights can I draw from my most difficult or hurtful experiences?
- What have I gained from having endured this experience?
- What am I grateful for?
- What actions do I need to take now to ensure that past pain does not block my current and future joy?

Identify your purpose and passions.

Ask yourself a few questions to get started:

- Do I have a clear purpose?
- If yes, what am I doing each day to fulfill it?
- If no, what can I do to expose myself to new experiences that might reveal my purpose to me?
- What issues am I passionate about?
- How have I encouraged my passions into my everyday life?

Reimagine and make the most of the time you have.

My experience with Lisa taught me to be more compassionate, particularly to single parents, who are working hard to balance their role of financial providers and caregivers. She taught me that to support parents I must first help them assess their evaluations of time. Through this relationship I have learned that many of us have more time than we realize. However, this truth is not immediately evident. We may, therefore, have to reimagine how we see time and how we organize our days. Furthermore, we have to make time and create more opportunities to discover and participate in the things that bring us joy. This will mean we have to prioritize our actions. When we say we want to do something, but don't have time, we may need to assess whether this is "real" or "imagined." Stepping out and trying that dream thing we want to try is scary, but reaching that achievement is made up of many steps along the way. Lisa used to think she did not have enough time to be a mom, to be physically active, and to fulfill her passion for traveling. But as of today, she has completed over 300 days of movement, she frequently travels with and without Amina, and she has an even busier schedule than she did five years ago. Once she reconceptualized time and started to use her resources wisely, she had more time. This is fundamentally the principle of balance and order.

Part III

What Is Her World?

7

Building Her Context and Valuing Heritage

Lisa's story reminds so many of us of our own because we are isolated and disconnected from who we are and from the experiences of those who came before us. Finding connections to ourselves and to our heritage can ground us, aid us in our parenting, and help us gain greater levels of joy.

When our girls are very young, our love feels like it's enough, but as they grow it becomes clear that they need the love and support of the greater community and the world around them. For that, they must learn to build their own safe space, their own village, and then they will feel safe to explore beyond those borders. So how do we help our girls navigate this?

We begin slowly. When children begin to feel the need for friends and gradually seek to belong to groups outside the family, moments arise when feelings of being loved and safe can be challenged. Sometimes those challenges are overt; other times they are subtle. Therefore, before your girl fully meets the world, you must help shape her feelings about herself before others can. You must be the first affirming voice inside her head.

Affirming your daughter's sense of self will increase her confidence, bolster her self-esteem, and enhance her feeling of belonging. As parents of a Black girl, Scott and I began this work by focusing on three core areas of our daughter's development: (1) knowledge of being unconditionally loved by her family, (2) belief in her own competence, and (3) respect for and knowledge of her African identity (as I discuss on page 87).

This chapter focuses on how context and heritage can anchor your girl to help her become more confident. I will talk about how teaching Marley respect for and knowledge of her African identity bolstered her sense of self. Scott and I worked hard to ensure that Marley knew that she was born of love and that we would love her no matter what. We taught her early on that she descended from creative, brilliant people, people who contributed to the creation of the world. We also invested resources to help her become competent, ensuring that she felt good about who she was, but also that she had the skills and information to do things that she wished to do. These three factors became the foundational pillars for her self-concept and the key features of her work as an activist.

Psychological research tells us that connecting children with their cultural and ethnic identities fosters emotional wellness. Embracing cultural identity builds self-esteem and self-efficacy. Adolescents with a strong regard for their ethnic group exhibit greater levels of daily happiness and less anxiety than children who lack this identification. Psychologists also agree that having a secure sense of racial identity is necessary to develop good self-esteem and superior coping abilities. It is not by chance that children with a strong ethnic identity perform better in schools than their peers without such strong affiliation. For children who are racial and ethnic minorities in the United States, embracing their ethnic identity can directly and indirectly affect well-being by buffering stressful experiences. Being able to draw on shared cultural belief systems is a vital resource that adolescents can use to deal with interpersonal struggles.

Of course, no parent can fully protect a child from every negative influence or attack, so we have had to coach Marley on dealing with what people say about who she is. For example, there was a time when she wore her hair in a large Afro. Students and teachers would comment directly to her in an interrogating, accusatory tone,

"Your hair is so big." The underlying questions were "Why is your hair so big?", "Why are you so visible?", and "Why are you taking up so much space in the world?"

One way that racism, sexism, and other inequities show up is in our interpersonal interactions with others, like the questions above that Marley was asked. These small unjust exchanges are referred to as *microaggressions.* Derald Wing Sue, professor of counseling psychology at Columbia University, defines microaggressions as "subtle snubs, slights, and insults directed toward minorities, as well as to women and other historically stigmatized groups, that implicitly communicate or at least engender hostility." Other scholars have suggested that we consider these actions as inadvertent racial or sexist slights. Microaggressions are particularly pernicious precisely because they usually occur in intimate exchanges between two or three people. Individuals who point out incidences of microaggression are often called hypersensitive. In some cases, people who report feeling victimized are faced with two seemingly difficult options: say nothing and risk becoming resentful or say something and be further victimized. If they say something, the person they have accused may deny engaging in discriminatory behavior and accuse them of being hypersensitive or paranoid. Such a response may mean that the person who was victimized is unlikely to report such incidents in the future. Because of this seeming double-bind, identifying and responding to microaggression demands having knowledge of self (know that your feelings matter), equity literacy (having the vocabulary to name the unjust thing that has happened), and an understanding of the situational context (identifying what was happening around you when the infringement occurred).

Microaggression can involve someone underestimating or overestimating one's behavior. It can make itself visible in sentences like "I didn't think people like you would know that" (underestimating) or "I thought since you were a girl you would know how to do that" (overestimating). Both statements reveal prejudicial ideas and assumptions. If you teach your girl that prejudice (bad ideas without foundation) and discrimination (unfair treatment because of those bad ideas), even when subtle, are unacceptable, she will have language to address these issues. We taught Marley to respond to these insulting probes by saying: "Yes, my hair is big, and I like it this way."

But her blunt and resolute response did not always stop these comments. When her hair was not the subject of consideration or conversation, her clothing, height, or even her glasses took center stage. "You are so tall," "Your glasses are green," "You are so smart" were typical comments. Each of these comments, though stated as benign and almost complimentary, was meant as an insult. The underlying assumption is that girls should not be tall—a sexist trope that serves to defeminize girls. Mentions of her green glasses can suggest that her creative expression in her eyewear is outside the normal standards. The suggestion is that she should conform. And like the comment on height, pointing out that she is smart is an attempt to isolate Marley, to label her as uncool.

These microaggressions are part and parcel of being a girl, especially a Black girl, in America's educational institutions. Though the literature on how Black girls experience primary and secondary educational settings—particularly the ways these experiences shape their mental well-being and sense of identity—is scant, sufficient data shows that racism organizes all children's lives in and out of school. In this respect, scholars like famed sociologist Eduardo Bonilla-Silva from Duke University have repeatedly found that racist structures—both overt and covert—shape our relationships on every level: They affect our position in the world socially, politically, economically, and ideologically. Therefore, comments like the ones teachers and students make to girls like Marley are part of a social racism practice that pervades school life. The phrase *social racism,* coined by sociologists Frances Henry and Carol Tator, describes the racialized language or discourse that manifests itself in euphemisms, metaphors, and omissions that support racist ideologies and policies.

Choosing to respond with "Thanks, I like it this way" is one way we have taught our daughter to diffuse racial stereotyping. We know that as a Black girl in a racially heterogenous environment where she is numerically and socially a minority, she can be quickly labeled as hostile and angry. The consequences of such a characterization are long felt and have penalties for her social relationships and her academic success. Dr. Monique Morris, author of *Pushout: The Criminalization of Black Girls in School,* chronicles the experiences of Black girls across the country. She found that Black girls who are characterized as angry are more likely to be unfairly disciplined in schools and have lower levels of achievement, and are less likely to receive academic support from teachers. Though these phrases may seem innocuous, they are part of a consistently subtle, yet hostile school space that makes Black girls like my daughter hyper self-conscious.

Having to come up with daily responses to these statements is a part of the race work and burden that all Black children have to do in integrated and white spaces. This race work involves defending their racial position and/or being spokespersons for their cultural/ethnic group. We urged our own daughter to be hyperaware of these daily assaults so that she does not allow them to define how she dresses, acts, or carries herself. At a very early age, we sought to have her understand that despite what was said or done, she was not the problem. The institutional space and the people around her who promoted, engaged in, or did nothing to stop this type of conventional behavior and inquiries were the real problem. I explicitly told her that though such persons might be considered nice, their behaviors promoted racist ideologies. Therefore, she had to observe what they did, not just what they said. She had to look for patterns in their behaviors that revealed or suggested that she and others like her were inferior. And when she saw these things, she had to reject their ideas.

World-renowned speaker and businesswoman Mellody Hobson, wife of filmmaker George Lucas, talks about the importance of being color-brave. In her 2004 TED Talk she distills sociological concepts about race and racism to help lay audiences find value in having conversations about race. I think we can learn a lot from this work. She argues, "Race in America makes people completely uncomfortable [and] bringing it up is like the conversational equivalent of touching the third rail." In her talk she draws on work by sociologists like Eduardo Bonilla-Silva. She says there is a tendency toward color blindness, which describes a learned behavior where we pretend not to notice race. She urges us to reject color blindness because it is very dangerous. Not talking about it means we're ignoring the problem. Discussing race and racism can be hard, awkward, and uncomfortable. But like Hobson, I agree that the goal is to become comfortable with being uncomfortable. And for would-be change-makers like your girl, it is essential that they confront challenges rather than avoid them. Issues of race are no different. But discussing race and racism means that as caregivers we have to become students of these concepts. We must understand that racism is about systems.

Racism is the web of ideas and actions that organizes our society. While discrimination is what occurs between people who we can identify and name, racism cannot necessarily be attached to a person. It is like a spider's web; it's tangled. We can see racism at work when we ask, Who are the rules benefiting? Who do the rules punish? Does everyone have an equal chance from birth to succeed? It is important that young children understand that racism begins with bad ideas (biases), and those bad ideas can lead to discrimination (bad actions that lead to us treating some people better than others). Racism becomes systematic—institutional—when those ideas are coupled with power and sources of power like money, military, police, school administrators, and teachers. The same is true for sexism and homophobia. The pathway begins with biases, becomes evident in discrimination, and then is perpetuated in systemic actions.

Managing our daughter's racial identity within this context was and is tricky work. As a sociologist, I am deeply familiar with literature arguing that embracing ethnic identity protects children from a host of deleterious health effects. I am fully cognizant that individuals with high levels of ethnic identity exhibit a high quality of life, a common indicator of well-being. We decided to ground Marley's identity in a pan-Africanist framework, one that connects her to the history of Africa and African-Americans while also valuing the genius and creativity of her Caribbean and Cape-Verdean ancestry.

We drew knowledge from scholars like Kobi Kambon from the University of Alabama at Birmingham, whose work shows that persons who feel connected to their African identity have a strong sense of self-determination but also recognize the power of the community. A pan-Africanist identity promotes harmony and spirituality and encourages individuals to work toward creating opportunities for the larger group, not just the self.

Unlike Marley, I was not raised with much knowledge about Africa, and truth be told, the Jamaicans I know do not like to be referred to as Africans. Indeed, I know lots of Black folk who hold the same anti-Black stereotypes as those promoted by white supremacists. We are all marinating in the same cultural soup filled with anti-Black ingredients.

Centering my child's identity in a pan-Africanist framework would demand that I learn more about African and African-American history, address my own anti-Black animus, be explicitly anti-racist, and foster a sense of peacefulness within our girl—all while making it abundantly clear to her that America is racist in every way all the time. Racism and oppression are always operating on multiple levels, simultaneously.

Choosing this path meant that Marley would need to understand some basic facts about the culture in which she was being raised. First, she needed to know that Africa is not a country, despite the efforts of the Western world to reduce it to that. Africa is a continent of many nations, cultures, and cultural practices; there is no singular African story, and by extension there is no singular way to be Black. It is also the birthplace of *all human life.* Second, African people's experiences are not singularly defined by the enslavement in the United States, South America, and/or the Caribbean. Societies existed before the rise and colonization of the West.

I knew that in schools Marley would be taught about the horrors that occurred in America from 1600 through the formal end of slavery in 1865, but I wanted her to know that while African people had been enslaved, we were not slaves. The distinction was critical: The former refers to a condition of forced labor, while the latter denies these captured people their humanity by making them synonymous with their subjugation. In fact, even after centuries of captivity and assault, people of African descent have survived and excelled. Moreover, these formerly enslaved people continue to contribute their genius to our lives.

Rather than teaching Marley abstract facts about Africa, Scott and I use our everyday life and the things around her to demonstrate the ways that the knowledge and creativity of African people positively impacts today's society. We have explained, for example, that Marley's ability to text her friends is largely owed to Dr. Shirley Jackson, the first African-American woman to earn a doctorate in nuclear physics at Massachusetts Institute of Technology, in 1973. In addition to her lengthy list of academic achievements, Jackson also has an impressive number of inventions under her belt. Her experiments paved the way for numerous developments in telecommunications, including the touch-tone telephone, caller ID, and call waiting.

We have also discussed the contributions of inventor Lewis Latimer, who collaborated with science greats Hiram Maxim and Thomas Edison. Latimer's carbon filament is a vital component of the creation of the lightbulb. He later collaborated with Alexander Graham Bell to draft the patent for Bell's design of the telephone. Latimer also designed an improved railroad-car bathroom, as well as an early air-conditioning unit.

It is vitally important to me that my girl understands that regardless of what is and isn't taught in schools, Black and African history is American history. Furthermore, whether we hail originally from Haiti, Jamaica, New Jersey, or Ohio, we all benefit from the contributions of people of African ancestry.

The first evidence that our teaching was taking hold came in an unexpected way. When Marley was six years old, one of her friends had a princess-themed birthday party. For weeks, clusters of excited six- and seven-year-old girls discussed which Disney princess they wanted to be. On the morning of the party, Marley merely said, "I want to wear a pretty dress." Without much thought, I helped her select a dress from her closet and did her hair. I was busy that afternoon, so Scott accompanied Marley to the princess party.

She returned home happy and reported having a great time. A few days later, a friend who had also been at the party walked up to me in our local supermarket. "Janice, what's up with your kid?" he asked. "She was the only girl at the party not dressed as a Disney princess." I didn't immediately respond, since I wasn't sure whether he was complaining or complimenting. He then described how some of the other girls had crowded around Marley and asked why she wasn't dressed as a princess. "I am," Marley told them. When they asked which princess, Marley responded, "I'm a Nubian princess, so everything I put on is princess clothing." I threw my head back and laughed. Nubia is a region along the Nile River near southern Egypt in central Sudan. Nubia was known as Kush for two thousand years. Though it is historically incorrect to say that all people of African descent are Nubians, I liked that Marley was connecting herself to the continent and to African people.

As a mother, I expect to make a lot of mistakes. Like every parent, I struggle to figure things out as I go. Our best bet is to get some things right, and to learn from what we get wrong. I put that Nubian princess story squarely in the column of getting things right.

Throughout her early years, though Marley continued to see herself as a Nubian princess, she was not singularly bound to any specific gender identity. Though we have made it clear the value of being connected with other girls—by virtue of their similar challenges and struggles—we did not push any specific gender schema onto her. We were cautious about the potential downsides of embracing specific gender norms. Additionally, we wanted to avoid the possibly harmful impact of any strict gender identity on her psychological functioning and well-being. Gender studies research cautions us that for some people, identifying with one gender more than the other can produce negative outcomes. That is, viewing the world through a specific gender lens may lead them to reject recreational, academic, or occupational options that might be perceived as gender-inappropriate, that is, as "not a girl thing." Therefore, adopting a specific gender schema may lead people to prove they are gender typical of their group, leading them to adopt exaggerated and even pathological aspects of same-gender roles.

Nonetheless, we chose to help her develop an intersectional identity. Feminist scholar Kimberlé Crenshaw argues that it is important to understand that for Black and brown girls their identities are intersectional. She defines *intersectionality* as the various ways race and gender interact to shape the multiple dimensions of Black women's and girls' experiences. Intersectionality theory seeks to illuminate the ways the experiences of Black women and girls cannot be understood within a narrow view of just gender or just race. Being a Black girl, then, means expanding the traditional boundaries of the way we see and understand race or gender. We cannot isolate these factors but rather need to see inequities associated with them as operating simultaneously.

In practice, this means making girls of color aware of the way everyday sexism and racism come together to shape their lives. I work with the GrassROOTS team to make our girls aware that they will likely experience sex stereotyping, whereby friends, family, educators, and others attribute a girl's abilities, motivations, behaviors, values, and roles to her sex, and her competency will often be questioned. Girls of all racial backgrounds need to be cautious about the gender games they play. *Gender*, like *race*, is a socially constructed term, and strong adherence to these concepts can trip us up.

To make sure that your girl doesn't lose her footing, you as a caregiver must be vigilant, and take action when necessary. From gender-based pay gaps to over-sexualized advertisements for childhood toys such as dolls with outsized eyes half the size of their faces and seductively puckered lips, girls are often treated as second-class citizens across the globe. Girls must be made aware that there is nothing wrong with them; it is the culture that is at fault. Further, girls must feel like they have the skills and talents enough to tackle these issues in their everyday lives. This often begins with debunking the mythologies told about girls with facts.

Developing a counter-narrative to the dominant one told to girls required that I become more aware of what occurs in schools. Scholars like Monique Morris, author of *Pushout*, helped here. To understand what was happening in schools, I had to talk to her and read more. Dr. Morris's work taught me that, regardless of socioeconomic context, African-American girls are negatively and differentially treated compared to their white peers. Teachers tend to focus on modifying social rather than academic skills of Black girls. Morris's research found that perceptions of Black girls by their teachers are largely based on their appraisal of students' femininity. Educators often focus their efforts on molding them into a particular model of womanhood.

Morris concluded that teachers engage in these behaviors because they perceive Black girl students as overly assertive or abrasive, lacking the "gender specific qualities associated with a 'well behaved' student"—such as "passivity," "silence," and being "deferential." These educators see their charge as an effort to "re-form the femininity of African American girls into becoming something more 'acceptable.'" To combat these inevitable attacks, I have spent the majority of my adult life helping girls and their caregivers negotiate these biases.

In my work, I advise girls to always conduct themselves in a cordial matter with regard to adults. But I also teach them to simultaneously reject ideas that seek to oppress them. Reject. Reject. Reject. I urge them to reject falsehoods about their culture, reject ideas that suggest they are inferior, and reject messages that suggest their point of view and feelings are not valid.

In practice, this model of rejecting oppression looks like this: taking a breath, pausing, and staying as calm as possible when faced with marginalizing experiences. I encourage a girl that if she is ever in doubt about what's happening, she should ask clarifying questions of her aggressor to help her understand their comments. For example: "I want to make sure that I understand what you were saying. Can you please help me understand what you meant by _____?" (She should insert the exact words the person used.)

When girls feel or observe themselves or someone around them being mistreated, they should report the incident with as much detail and as many facts as possible by saying, "I noticed that you did this . . ." Lastly, I encourage them to share with adults exactly how they feel about the situation, because it is important that they know that their feelings about inequity matter.

At GrassROOTS we are in consistent dialogue about terms like *race* and *gender*. As a sociologist, I know that these words and concepts are often difficult and/or misused. Trying to explain these words to girls and, further, trying to help them see and understand how they are used in everyday life demands creativity because sometimes their parents do not understand the terms. And worse yet, sometimes their parents have given them bad information about these terms.

I work hard to make sure the girls understand that *race* and *gender* are terms people use to organize the world. They are not biological or natural; they can be changed and mean different things depending on where we go in the world. Sociologists call these terms social constructions because they are constructed for use in our society. These terms are unnatural, human-made, and hold no inherent truth or value. Our decision to call ourselves Black or White is for social convenience.

We are descendants of Africa. Africa is a place, yet we call ourselves Black because that is the shared term some people of African descent use to connect and relate to others. Our skins are not actually black or white, but we use the term to identify people from different geographies. In the case of Black, not everyone likes this term. Some people like African-American; some like Jamaican, some Brazilian, and some French. We respect people's right to call themselves whatever they wish. We acknowledge Africa as the birthplace and respect the differences that exist among all people whose families started life on the continent.

In America, race determines who gets resources and who does not, and the same is true with gender. To help the girls understand how both these things influence their everyday lives, I ask them to tell me who they think has the most power in the United States. Who gets to decide the rules? Their first answer is always adults. And they are correct. Older people have more money and decision-making power than children or younger adults. Then I ask them to drill down on what type of people have the most power. They are quick to identify that white (European) men and boys do. Their examples often come from their school experiences with countless examples of how boys get away with doing things wrong while teachers are quick to punish girls. They can recall a myriad of incidents where girls, regardless of race, are not given as much space to make mistakes as boys are.

Usually our girls have an instinct that racism or sexism is happening around them, and they want support to know they are not being crazy for feeling that something is wrong with what is being said or done. They usually are searching for words to describe what they observe or experience. They typically say something like, "I know it's wrong, but my teacher and the school did nothing about it." The "it" varies from boys pulling girls' hair to white kids asking Black kids for the N-word pass.

It is important that your girl understands that some people who support racist systems can also be "nice" people. Racism is not always overt, and people who endorse systems of inequality do not always say bad or mean things. They can sometimes say nothing and allow a bad thing to happen. Dr. Camara Jones describes this as inaction in the face of need. If we do not make it clear that racism is not about nice people and not-so-nice people, we run the risk of confusing our children and making it hard for them to understand why some nice people can still engage in and support oppressive behaviors.

We must make it clear to our girls that racism continues to exist because we often treat it like it is natural or biological and assume there is nothing we can do about it. As parents, we must learn and help our children see that racism was created; it's unnatural, human-made. That means it can be undone, but only if people act to end it. Children and parents must learn to become anti-racist agents of change. Such actions often begin by teaching our girls how to identify and respond to microaggressions.

For example, Beth and Zane both attend an integrated neighborhood school. At one of our SuperGirls Society meetings, we were talking about common challenges they face at school. Though they were in separate classes, both girls told stories of their teachers' actions toward them. They reported that when their white friends are happy, their teachers typically say things like "You seem so happy today." But when Beth or Zane are happy and jovial, their teachers never say anything—although when they are tired or frustrated, their teachers make comments like, "You look mad today." The girls noted the imbalance in the teachers' comments. Their happiness goes unnoticed, and their tiredness gets amplified and marked as anger. Though our SuperGirls come from various school districts, there was a chorus of shared agreement. One SuperGirl remarked, "It's like they are looking for our problems." Looking for problems was quite an elucidating comment for me. Girls are very aware of the racial patterns in teachers' actions. Some responses show up as erasure through color blindness (more about this later), and other behaviors show up through stereotyping.

Girls need to understand the insidious ways that race and racism organize and shape their daily lives. Similarly, they need to understand what sex and gender are, and how these concepts (and how they are interpreted) influence their daily lives. Girls must learn that their sex is determined by their biological assignment at birth, but their family often decides their gender; as they grow they may choose a different gender expression than the one assigned at birth.

Sexism is radically easier for all the girls to identify than racism. They see it everywhere, but it is amazingly clear in their schools' dress codes. Each year our girls launch complaints about the fact that they cannot wear tank tops at school even when it's hot and how happy they are that they can wear whatever they want to at camp. Middle-school girls are the most animated in how much they dislike their schools' dress codes. To them it is clear that the rules were written to manage girls' bodies and to make sure their existence does not make boys and men teachers uncomfortable.

When girls raise these issues, my role is to help them make sense of the fact that these rules were created by people, and for that reason they should feel excited. Written or created rules mean that they can be rewritten and re-created. Unlike our biology, which takes a long time to change, human-made rules give us a chance to enact change. The first time they hear me say this they think I am crazy, but over the course of the years with me they come to see the power in created rules.

Another critical part of my role is to make sure girls know that there is nothing wrong with them if they feel angry or frustrated. They should not have to perform happiness for others. Furthermore, there is nothing wrong if their shirts, dresses, or pants hug their bodies. The gender and race rules are a part of compliance systems to put them in their assumed subordinate place. I call these rules "attempts to restrict your humanity." They don't have to like and they don't have to accept them. They can choose to reject and rebel against them.

To this end, I ask them to do a few things. Make a list of how often they see these unfair rules. Check to make sure they are not also enforcing these oppressive rules. Are you telling girls how they should be or how they should dress? Are you saying or suggesting to other Black kids that there is only a certain way to be Black? It is important to me that they know that they have one of two roles in the system—uphold the unjust rules or work to end them.

But to change the rules, girls will need a strong sense of their own competency. The racist-sexist infrastructure of society not only assaults girls' self-esteem—their feelings about themselves—but it undermines girls' belief in their capabilities to organize, execute, and create change in certain situations. As caregivers you must do all that you can to reinforce girls' self-esteem and help them remain self-efficacious.

ASSIGNMENTS

Equip her with an awareness of her heritage and the contributions of people from her cultural ancestry.

Whether she is African-American, African, Middle Eastern, Eastern European, Asian, Irish, or anything in between, educate her on her heritage. Find the positive qualities of her cultural ancestry. Research the world around you. Make sure she understands her history—the good, the bad, and the ugly.

Identify the contributors who shaped your daughter's world, in both big and small ways.

A sense of history will give her a sense of her possibility. If you can, try to find local examples. For example, in our town alone we found:

- Marie Van Brittan Brown, despite working full-time as a nurse, devised an early burglar alarm system that would alert her to strangers at her door and contact relevant authorities as quickly as possible.
- Garrett A. Morgan patented the mechanical traffic light in 1923 and sold it to General Electric.
- Madam C. J. Walker invented beauty products for Black women's hair.

You can start on the Internet, but, even better, take her to the library to see what books and films you might discover together.

Learn and talk to her about race and gender.

Talk to your girl and help her use these strategies for dealing with microaggression.

Make the invisible visible.
Let her know that if a person does something that makes her feel emotionally or physically unsafe, she should let them know immediately. Let her know that silence will not save her.

Articulate concern.
Ask her to voice her concern to that person and to those around her who care for her—like you. The practice of speaking truth to power begins in these intimate exchanges. Girls

need words to voice their concerns. As a caregiver, you should equip her with an equity vocabulary so that she can feel comfortable saying phrases like:

- "When you do [insert upsetting action or thing] or say [insert upsetting action or thing], it hurts my feelings."
- "I have asked you not to do [insert upsetting action or thing] because it is clearly not true, and yet you keep doing it."
- "Please do not [insert upsetting action or thing] that way; it makes me uncomfortable."

Don't assume intent; focus on your feelings.

Prejudicial ideas are pervasive, and people can engage in actions of which they are unaware. They may reflexively and unconscientiously do or say harmful things. They may repeat things that they have heard others say without realizing that those comments are problematic. Girls should not assume that people know that what they are doing is harmful. The one thing girls need to know for sure is how they feel. Girls need to know that their feelings are valid. Those feelings matter and should be expressed.

List and identify patterns of bad behavior.

Persistent bad behaviors that harm others should not be labeled as microaggression. If your girl experiences *consistent* mistreatments, she should make note of the bad behaviors and report them to a trusted person in charge. Regular and ubiquitous hurts are not small matters (micro), they are large (macro). You and your girl should demand macro-level responses from people in authority, such as school administrators or the police.

8

Freely Offer Your Critique

~~~~~~

The work of teaching your girls to challenge unjust and inequitable rules begins at home. Show them that having a point of view is essential for taking action, and that offering critique is valuable for her personal growth and critical thinking. You can do this work by helping your girl understand herself within a larger context, but always start with the small things around her. Seek out answers to questions like: What does she value? Who are her people, both family and friends? Does she have a solid crew? Is she making good choices and building herself a village that supports and energizes her? Answering these questions will help you understand her values and provide you with information on how best you can help her grow bearing equity in mind. Said differently, if you want to raise a change-maker you must model for her, and one way you can do that is to freely and frequently offer your critique.

When I'm hanging out with Marley, I don't hold back on calling things out. I call out unfairness or dubious morality. I critique television shows, popular songs, YouTube videos, pop culture personalities, and even Marley's friends as well as my friends and family. It's my responsibility to raise flags about anyone or anything that might promote inequity, plant seeds of distrust, embrace conspicuous consumption, and ultimately encourage self-loathing in my child. That usually means it's open season on music with gratuitous sexism, violence, classism, and profane angst; television shows with rude or overly precocious kids; friends who seem shady; and parents, celebrities, and politicians who don't exhibit integrity. Nothing and no one is off-limits. I am an equal opportunity critic.

I don't always expect Marley to give up the people and entertainments she enjoys, but in the cases I deem to be non-negotiable, I explain fully why I'm asking her to forgo her engagement. And I'm not just trying to annoy my daughter; I am trying to manipulate her. Yes, you heard me right. *Manipulate.* Not the kind of manipulation you may think of. No, I am not seeking to control or unfairly take advantage of her, but rather I am trying to artfully and skillfully mold her into a healthy skeptic, with a solid moral center. I want her to vigorously analyze her world and her influences. I also want to limit her access to unhappy, pessimistic, and oppressive people, as well as unimaginative and fearful people—what the hippies might call toxic negativity. It's real, and it can be deeply damaging.

Each day I tackle something or someone new. With roughly sixteen years to raise my daughter, I can pick and choose who and what to be critical of each day. One of my favorite targets is disloyal friends. Teenagers are passionate about their friends, so as a parent I'm invested in Marley making solid selections. Her social circle is going to shape what she does, where she goes, and who she's going to be around for years to come, so why would I want her surrounded by people who don't really value her, who aren't interested in what matters to her, or who might be involved in activities that are harmful to her well-being? If a girl has been carefully nurtured, she will know what kindness and compassion feel like, and she will be able to tell when people don't operate from these values. Every girl will at some point have a friend who is a little suspect. In such cases, I suggest that you offer your scathing critique, but do it in a way your child can hear.

Say there's someone in your child's life who exhibits some mean-girl tendencies. Maybe you ask your girl: "Do you think Jasmine says nice things about you when you're not around? What do you value most about your friendship? Are you prepared to reconsider this friendship if you think it is causing you harm?" You aren't saying she needs to stop being friends with this person, but you want her to think about the relationship and draw some conclusions of her own.

When Marley was five, a friend handed her a note that said, "Marley is ugly and dumb." The note had been written by a classmate who apparently did not like my child. This classmate gave the note to one of Marley's closest friends, let's call her Bianca, who then read the note, laughed, and passed it along to Marley. That night, Marley showed me the note. She insisted she wasn't upset. "I am not dumb, and I am not ugly," she said, "so it doesn't bother me, Mommy." But the note bothered *me*. I wasn't so concerned about the girl who wrote the note, because that child was not Marley's friend. Far more upsetting was that Bianca read the note, laughed, and then passed it on! I remarked to Marley that these were not the actions of a good friend. I also reached out via phone to Bianca's mom about the situation. Bianca conceded that perhaps the note should not have been shared, but neither mother nor daughter thought it was a big deal. "They're just being kids," Bianca's mother told me, dismissing the whole affair. For me, their lack of remorse was a deal breaker.

Now comes the hard part. Even though I really wanted Marley to end the friendship, Marley liked Bianca a lot and resisted. As the more forgiving of the two of us, she argued that Bianca had meant no harm and would know better in the future. Darn it, I had successfully instilled in my daughter the value of forgiveness and patience, looking for the best in people and giving folks a chance. Now I had to abide by the very philosophies I had taught her. In the end, forgiveness and patience won. *But*—big caveat—Marley and I had several in-depth conversations to develop criteria for what positive friendship looks like. At the end of this chapter, I am going to ask you to do the same exercise.

When it comes to television and social media, you bet I don't censor my critiques. Don't get me wrong—I enjoy them both. I have spent many weekends watching movie after movie. However, I loathe commercials. Too many episodic children's shows are filled with advertisements that promote terrible values.

When Marley was young, I had a list of shows that I despised. The show *Jessie* was easily top of the list. It was one of the most problematic shows of the prime Disney Channel era. The premise was simple: Two wealthy Hollywood stars adopt several children from the world and hire a nanny, Jessie, to care for them because they are too busy to take care of the children themselves. Although the show had a racially diverse cast, the characters represented a series of racial, gender, and economic stereotypes. The lead characters included a sassy Black immigrant girl, Zuri; a smart Indian boy, Ravi; a charming and sarcastic biracial boy, Luke; and an unmotivated and vain blond girl, Emma. Each episode had a moral lesson intended to educate its youthful viewers, but that ambitious charge did not overshadow the show's core flaw—the promotion of bigotry. Most of Ravi's jokes were built around him being an unpopular nerd who did not understand American culture, thereby advancing the image of the uncultured immigrant and promoting the idea that smart is uncool. Zuri, the Ugandan girl, never spoke about her culture; her jokes mainly focused on her judgments of others. She was often scolded for being mean and having an attitude. In each episode she had to be taught to "be nice"—yet another example of the overused, tired trope of the angry Black girl. Luke loved video games, dancing, and causing mischief—classic image of a future frat boy. Emma, the only birth child of the parents, flaunted her wealth and did not care about school. She was mainly regarded as the "dumb blonde." Jessie, their main caretaker, was considered a hick from rural America who would do anything to please her wealthy benefactors. The show drove me mad, but Marley loved it, and I compromised; she had to endure watching it with me and listening to my running dialogue about all the problematic themes.

I could not be quiet because I know that media can affect children's self-esteem. The education literature has countless studies illustrating that children (especially heavy television viewers) will likely adopt the belief that boys are dominant, assertive, and powerful because these are the perspectives most frequently seen on television. Social identity theory predicts that boys use these characteristics themselves as a basis of comparison to maintain their self-concept. Heavy watchers of television may be more likely to believe that girls are passive, weak, and insignificant. These stereotypic media portrayals can lead to a negative self-evaluation among girls.

Concerned about the impact of television on Marley's self-concept, Scott and I were very particular about what shows she could watch. The resolution: If she was interested in watching TV, we were going to watch it with her. Over the years, I have spent many hours watching shows with my daughter, and without fail, I continually point out some of the more common racist and sexist tropes, especially in comedic series and commercials. When she started elementary school, she wanted to watch more television than she had previously watched. So we made allowances. Scott and I made it a point to watch with her the first three episodes of every show she was interested in. We wanted to get a firm grasp on the content of these shows to better understand her interests. If the show was minimally problematic, she could watch it without supervision. If she loved a show and it had things in it that we found objectionable, then we would decide to watch it with her or simply say no. *SpongeBob SquarePants* was not an option at all. She was not allowed to watch that show. The show chronicles the adventures of SpongeBob and his aquatic friends in the fictional underwater city of Bikini Bottom. The adult humor and unabashed profanity made it fully inappropriate for young children. *Jessie* was troublesome but we allowed it. As with all things, we reserved the right to decide and to change our minds if we felt like she understood why some shows were troublesome and others were not. As she got to middle school, we allowed her to watch some shows on her own, but we still carefully monitored her choices. By then we had identified and discussed many of the damaging themes that are often woven through stories developed for children. Here are a few of the consistent tropes we discovered:

- Overweight girls usually chase boys for affection, thereby sending the message that being overweight equals being desperate.

- Black boys are generally cast as dancers or athletes. The message: Black boys exist to perform for others.
- Kids spend the majority of their time begging for or wanting to acquire some object, which subversively promotes excessive consumerism.
- Friendships often involve deception and talking behind people's backs, reinforcing the idea that friendships built on lies and duplicity are acceptable.

As you can imagine, there were many shows Scott and I decided were off-limits. And for a long time Marley was limited to just one hour of television on a school night. She was always welcomed to watch the news with us, though she seldom took us up on that offer. On weekends, we invited her to watch movies with us, even those that featured fantastical violence, but we drew the line at shows in which women or girls were sexually and physically assaulted. As a family, we avoided the constant interruption and problematic messaging of commercials altogether, choosing mostly to tape her favorite shows on DVR or watch them through a subscription network like Netflix.

In case you are wondering, of course Marley is often irritated by my constant analyzing and critiquing of media, which inevitably meant that some of the more popular series would never be played in our home. And, no, she couldn't watch them at Grandma's or a friend's house either. I was crystal clear with the grandparents, aunties, and friends about what was and was not acceptable while Marley was in their care. My critique was liberally shared with all people who hosted Marley.

Asking grandparents to observe your parenting boundaries can be especially tricky. My mother recognizes that I am *particular*—that's the word my family applies to me—about how Marley engages with the world. Knowing that I am opinionated about what is developmentally appropriate and healthy for my child, my mother does not care to provoke my displeasure. Scott's mom, on the other hand, worried that Marley would be a "weirdo" because of the intentional way we were raising her.

I'm aware that my approach to parenting can draw criticism. So, fair warning: When you opt out of what is popular and known, you might be cast as an oddball. There will also be times when you question yourself and wonder if others are right. Are you being *too* particular? Is this fair to your girl? What's wrong with her watching the popular shows, if everyone is watching them? Maybe a TV in her room is okay? Maybe I am being too harsh or judgmental about some shows? In truth, it's normal and healthy to regularly revisit the boundaries you've set for your child, adjusting what is and isn't allowed as she grows into new developmental stages. But these re-evaluations must come from you, not from an outside chorus. It helps if you can actively create a community of parents who will remind you that being the *particular* parent not only serves your child, but ultimately contributes to the betterment of our society.

Decisions about when to get a phone and whether your child should be on social media are among the issues that often showcase the differences between your parenting practice and others'. Some parents are clear that children under thirteen should not have phones or be allowed access to social media. COPPA, the Children's Online Privacy Protection Act, states that any organizations or people operating online services (including social media services) are not allowed to collect the personal information of anyone under the age of thirteen without parental permission. Further, there are a growing number of concerns about the impact of social media usage on children's well-being. The research evidence in this area is mixed and the causal order remains unclear. Scholars have not been able to discern whether social media usage produces certain outcomes or whether certain types of children are more susceptible to particular behaviors because of their use of social media. One set of studies has found that there are many benefits of using online technologies, including increased self-esteem, perceived social support, increased social capital, safe identity experimentation, and increased opportunity for self-disclosure. Others maintain that social media has many harmful effects such as increased exposure to harm, social isolation, depression, and cyber-bullying. Caregivers should weigh their decisions carefully, and in the end, their choices should be based on their values and their understanding of their children.

Marley got a phone at nine years old. Admittedly, I didn't think she needed a phone since she was primarily with us and we had phones. She spoke to us and family and we had no need for independent communication. But one day, on a rare occasion, I needed help with Marley and asked a parent to pick her up from school for me. I told the parent that I would pick Marley up at six o'clock. I arrived at the mom's house at six, but no one was home, so I called. I got no response. I waited for five minutes and called again. No response. I then called again every five minutes. One hour passed before the mom returned and I was able to take Marley home. In that time, I was in a full state of panic. I vowed that would never ever happen again. I would always be able to reach my child. I talked with Scott, who was eligible for an upgrade for his phone. We agreed that Marley would have his old phone and he would get an upgrade. We sat with her and explained the basic rules of the phone. She was to always have it on (vibrate during school and ringer after school) and with her. She was not to use it during the school day and could not use it until her homework was complete. Because most of her friends did not have phones, she was not overly enamored with the phone. She used it to play games and watch YouTube videos. At night, the phone was kept downstairs out of her room or across from her on her desk. She used it for emergencies only. Things continued that way until she got to seventh grade.

At eleven years old, after her #1000BlackGirlBooks campaign became popular, she was allowed to join Instagram. Because Scott and I have avidly used Facebook since its inception and I had great facility with phones, using them sometimes more often than my computer, we were familiar with these media. We are also pretty tech savvy. I love memes, GIFs, and short-cut keys. Consequently, we had a good sense of the world she was entering. I had also managed GrassROOTS' social media online and wrote for our monthly newsletter, so I knew that the smallest sentence could be misconstrued and people could feel comfortable being hostile to others from the comforts of their keyboards.

The decision to allow her into such a big space filled us with some dread. Racists and predators can be anywhere, but it felt like they were everywhere on the Web. We knew they would eventually find her, and we were going to have to equip her with skills to still thrive even in what seemed like a hostile space. We outlined the rules for her. She was allowed to use the account between 3:00 and 7:00 P.M. Her dad and I had her password, and we shadowed her account. We could tell when she logged in; we could see all the messages sent to her and her responses. Furthermore, we had a public relations team who was monitoring Marley's social media account.

The simplest rule was for the posts themselves: Only post and look at things that Grammy—Scott's mother, Joann—would approve of. Joann has very strict standards of decorum; therefore, she is a good barometer for what to do. Very early on we didn't realize how much work allowing our child on social media would demand of us. We needed to consume way more information about popular culture than we really wanted to. We had to learn the slangs, the latest games, who and what were en vogue and what wasn't. It is here that I often find that parents opt out. Irritated that social media has brought so much of the outside into their child's life, they try to push it out. They don't mediate or try to mitigate the impact; they evade. But evasion will not work. Mitigation has proven to be a better route. I suggest all parents sit with their children and decide on the social media and phone rules of engagement. Collectively, you can set up the acceptable length of time for usage, code of conduct, and penalty for violation of those rules. Write them down and use them as a way to address the inevitable challenges that will occur.

Admittedly, I dislike lots of the popular music, people, and things that my kid likes, but I am almost fifty years old. I am not supposed to. She gets to like what she likes, but as a young girl, she does not get to do what she wants to do. So it's fine if she likes mumble rap and scantily clad men, women, and boys, but I get to decide when and under what conditions she gets access to such information.

Much like the television shows, rather than simply hating on her stuff with little or no information, I had to become familiar with it.

Scott was a great partner in this. He is much more willing to watch and engage with her and even summarizes for me the shows she likes on YouTube. He even learns the latest dances and lingo; he knows Snapchat and TikTok while I better understand Twitter and Facebook. However, he is also more overprotective than I am, so if he hated something, then I had to see it to become the mediator between him and Marley. If there was an impasse between them, I would serve as the tie-breaker. Most of the time I sided with Marley, but I understood Scott's position. Marley wrote an article about us on these issues titled "Parents Just Don't Understand." In it she describes the ways we, mostly Scott, censor her music and television viewing. It was a great article, but we remain resolute that until we are fully convinced that she will make great decisions without our guidance, we will continue to actively insert our voices where necessary.

So here is my advice to parents: Teach your girl to exercise good judgment. But know that good judgment comes through trial and error. Also, this means you have to give her concrete examples of where the line is so that she knows when she crosses it. It is not a matter of if she will cross it; it is when. Why is one decision good and another unwise? Under what conditions can she do x but not y? These things must be explicitly spelled out to her. And even after you have laid them out, still have to provide governance and oversight.

In Marley's case, if she wanted to post on social media, she had to get approval. We continued this practice until she turned fifteen. Though we continue to provide some oversight, social media has expanded, and her knowledge and skills have far surpassed ours. Her exchanges online are often out of our purview, and as I am sure you can imagine, she has done her fair share of dumb things online. Luckily, they have not led to any long-term harm for her, and even better we know a lot of equally adept caregivers and children who can keep us informed if and when she crosses the line.

Though we are concerned about values, we are also worried about access to false information. We continue to remind Marley and all the SuperGirls that not all information on the Web is trustworthy. More often than not, I find myself repeating some of what technology strategist Luvvie Ajayi argues in her blog: "5 Things to Do to Avoid Passing on Fake News on Social Media." Whether it's celeb news or world news, it is important to "Click the post and read beyond the headline"; consider the timing of stories by always looking at the date. And always asks yourself, "Is this information current?" When in doubt, Google it. As Luvvie maintains: If you read something that seems outrageous, before you pass it on to others, pause and Google it. Find a second or third source.

Whether it is information on the latest celebrity breakup or who won a political office, social media usage is about values and the ability to make discerning choices. Be sure that your girl has demonstrated good judgment and is guided by your family's values *before* she has a phone or gets online. This will be especially valuable as she interacts with more and more people. Note: Other parents will judge you for these decisions. So for this reason and more, you need to find your tribe, a group of parents who will support and respect your boundaries and honor your values.

I know it can be hard, especially when other parents don't respect your choices or your approach to parenting. And that's going to happen. Some parents will outright disagree with your parenting choices—and they will be fairly easy to avoid—but others will try to hide their judgments; even your loved ones will not always see eye to eye. Usually disagreements occur when you don't do what someone else does or what someone else wants you to; know that it is okay. You are parenting a change-maker, and change-makers have to be able to endure critiques.

I learned the lesson the hard way when Marley was in preschool. She befriended a girl I'll call Kira. Kira was a delicate child who became easily upset and cried all the time. Marley would console her. They became fast buddies, often hanging out together after school. Over time, the small circle of two girls grew to five. The girls carried on like this for several years.

Playdates were usually held at Kira's. Her house was large and had a finished basement. Kira's family was significantly wealthier than the rest of us, and her mother—I'll call her Carla—was a stay-at-home parent. Carla supplied unlimited Costco juices and snacks. The girls played downstairs while we mothers gathered in the kitchen, sharing tales of family and life. It seemed like a fine arrangement until one day at the end of the playdate, as I was driving home with Marley, she mentioned that Kira had been mean to her. Marley didn't want to go to her house anymore. I was surprised and asked her why.

"She's fine when it's just us, but when other kids are around she is mean to me," Marley explained.

"What does she say or do that is mean?" I asked, keeping my tone neutral. Marley and Kira seemed like good friends, and I wondered if my daughter was exaggerating.

"She makes fun of me for not having stuff she has and she makes fun of the things I like," Marley insisted. "She's mean."

I took that in.

"Did you tell her to stop being mean?"

"Yes, I did, but that doesn't stop her," she responded.

So I said, "Okay, Marley, I hear you. Let me talk to her mom."

I felt quite comfortable calling Carla because we had become friends; I expected we would talk through what occurred at her house, get verification for Marley's story, and if needed develop a course of action to resolve any conflicts. I thought this would be a quick and easy talk and that we would come to a speedy solution. I assumed that whatever occurred was likely just a misunderstanding between the girls that we as caregivers could help mediate with some open communication. As it turned out, this was not the case. Carla verified the story, but her assessment was that "Marley needs to toughen up."

I was surprised by this response. Her reaction fit neither with my past experience nor with research on the matter. In a study by the Society for Research in Child Development called "Parent and Peer Contexts for Moral Reasoning Development," researchers noted that infants understand harm and fairness, though it can take children years before they apply this understanding to their own interactions with others. That is why I believe it is incumbent upon parents to actively encourage their children to act considerately toward their peers. I assumed we both abhorred children making fun of each other, but after hearing that Carla was unwilling to intercede, even though Kira had been mean to Marley, I acquiesced to my daughter's wish to no longer have playdates with Kira.

You see, our children know very clearly what feels injurious and unjust to them. This is another reason why we must create relationships with them so they feel comfortable sharing their true feelings with us. In Kira's case, I shared with Carla that my daughter would no longer hang out with her daughter, but we would see each other around the neighborhood. We remained cordial and continued our lives separately. Marley felt relieved about no longer having to spend time with a girl who did not appear to value her, yet she held no hard feelings. If this seems like an outcome too drama-free, too good to be true, it is. If only we adults could be like kids and move on like them without malice. I am not young, so I still felt irritated, and wholly surprised, by Carla's response, but not enough to begrudge her. The values difference, though I knew it existed, occurred spontaneously, and I was not really prepared for her response. Though my uncomfortable feelings about the situation would abate, it made me more cautious around her.

Fast-forward to years later. Carla wanted Kira to join the Grass-ROOTS SuperCamp. Marley was excited to see Kira; whatever previous conflict they'd experienced seemed to be long forgotten. I, however, was still cautious. Carla had a way of inserting her economic position into all conversations, and I was concerned that she might behave similarly at camp. With some trepidation on my part, Kira joined SuperCamp. Our camp serves girls of various incomes. Some families are supported by state subsidies, while others are affluent, some even more well-off than Carla. Celebrities' and government officials' children attend the camp.

As it happened, Kira's birthday and party fell during the summer training, and Carla chose to invite only those girls from the program whose families were financially well-off. Marley was invited, but chose not to go. I had not been aware that Carla had invited only the rich kids. She had merely informed me that her daughter was leaving early because it was her birthday. Marley knew the full story and told me who was invited, pointing out that only certain girls got an invite. It was Marley, at nine years old, who quietly perceived that economic class lines had been drawn. I can only guess that she saw this invitation as problematic and didn't want to harm or alienate the other girls. Luckily, other families were not aware, and the incident occurred without causing a disruption. I did not address the incident with Carla because I had no solution to offer. The party occurred, other families were not aware, and I was confident that no matter what, I did not want her back at camp the next year.

Several months later, after camp had ended, I learned that Kira was being bullied at school. Worse, no one had come to her aid. Even though she and Marley now attended different schools, I reached out to Carla, offering my sympathies and support. I knew how it felt when Marley was bullied. Surprisingly, she sounded more angry than hurt. She responded by saying, "One day these kids will be working for my kid." I was irritated and clicked off the call, saddened all over again by her lack of understanding of kids' emotional needs and her assumption that money can solve issues of inequity.

Carla's angered response, which may have come from a place of hurt, calls to mind a perspective sometimes found among well-resourced parents. Too often, some parents opt for covering up troubling idiosyncrasies or bad behavior in their offspring with phrases like, "Our kids are going to be fine." The assumption is that these childhood flaws will magically disappear by the time children reach adulthood. We mistakenly believe that because we, their parents, have achieved some financial stability and provided our children with a solid education, we can parent on autopilot and all will be well. As a parent and sociologist, I completely reject this idea. Our children will not be okay unless we explicitly and intentionally help them to develop into healthy, caring adults. To that end, it is our charge to help create a space for them to be joyful and contributing members of society.

For me, the circumstances surrounding Kira's situation served as a poignant example of why we must be active, intentional parents.

We must teach our children the importance of kindness toward others. All the money in the world cannot save a child whose spirit has been impaired. Though the story is not yet complete, the case of Carla and Kira is a cautionary one. It highlights the ways caregivers are sometimes complicit in promoting social and class divisions. Because Kira's mom did not address issues of unkindness when it was directed at someone else's child, my daughter, she was not able to understand how her daughter might feel when the same unjust actions were taken toward her.

I know some of you might see what happened to Kira as karma. I do not. I see it as an example of what happens if children adopt bad behaviors. I wholeheartedly agree with Dr. Kenneth Nunn, who in his paper titled "Bullying" in the *Journal of Pediatrics and Child Health* argues that bullies emerge within systems that bully. He maintains that the glorification of bullying behavior in the adult population is endemic within the media, the business culture, and families; therefore we should not be surprised when children bully. Bullying is an adult-created problem. Rather than taking the laissez-faire approach to acts of bullying and overlooking the dynamics that occur within children's friendships, parents should freely offer critique and interrupt bad behaviors, opting instead to help their girls build a social network of people who affirm them and allow them to flourish.

ASSIGNMENTS

Check your hater compass.

There's a difference between being a *hater* and being a *critic*. Be careful that as you offer your critique, you are not becoming a hater. Critiques are constructive; offering critique begins with asking questions to better understand the source of disagreement. Giving critique means you must be open to the potential of error, and you must be willing to be critiqued. Hating is always destructive. It aims to tear down rather than build up. Haters value silence and devalue questions. They tell rather than ask; they are dogmatic without reason. Those who offer critique will seek to provide solutions, and as parents they will always focus on the well-being of all children. They are willing to provide resources to address challenges and to participate in remediation. Hater parents are focused on their own satisfaction with little thought to children's well-being; they compare children, often pitting one against another. They do not acknowledge other children's strengths and overlook their own children's areas of challenges. They are generally unwilling to actively participate in finding solutions.

Share your opinions on *everything.*

I bet you are excited about this one. Once you've checked your hater compass, don't hold back; let your critiques fly! Girls need to know whom to trust and whom not to trust and why, and to understand how your values operate in practice. I mean, keep it relevant and on point, but you should make clear what principles you struggle with and why. Their friends *are* a conversation piece. Studies show that kids develop their moral center not by Socratic methods but by grappling with real moral dilemmas. Make sure your girl is secure enough in your relationship to use you as a sounding board.

Spend time with your children's friends and their parents.

Peers have a huge influence on your girl's sense of self; therefore, you need to know her friends and the people raising them. Invite her friends' parents to lunch or, if they are never free, develop a texting relationship with them. When their children are with you, send them pictures and ask that they do the same when yours are with them. The warmth you share with these families will enhance communication and relationships.

Build those bridges. As a relationship grows, perhaps let your daughter bring a close friend along on a weekend vacation and/ or invite her close friend's family along.

Develop criteria for what positive friendship looks like.

- Using a used tissue box or one that you can find at a local crafts shop, decorate and design your own friendship box. You can use paint, ribbons, crayons, or anything you like. Make it as beautiful as possible.
- Find some cardstock paper or plain index cards. Grab some multicolored markers, crayons, or Sharpies.
- With your girl, brainstorm ten qualities of a good friend. Each quality gets its own card. On one side, write and define the quality that matters to you. On the other side, provide up to three examples of each attribute. Be as specific as possible. You can also choose to decorate the card.
- Put your cards in the box and keep them handy for reflection and for those hard times when friendship conflict occurs.

Teach her to take stock of her friendships.

It is not easy deciding who to let in and let go of in your life. But making those hard decisions is critical in the journey of finding and sustaining a joyful life. Here are some questions your girl can consider as she makes these choices:

- How does this person contribute to or enrich my life?
- Does this person complement me and/or help me grow emotionally?
- What would be absent from my life if they were gone?
- Would their absence create an emotional challenge for me?
- In what ways am I made better through my relationship with this person?

Watch programs and listen to music together with your children.

If you allow them to watch television, use the computer, or listen to music online, make sure you are fully familiar with what they are consuming. Do not critique from ignorance. Explicitly articulate what you like and what you object to and why. Offer them an opportunity to present a counter-narrative and even help them make a case for why they may like something that you do not. A major caveat: Do *not* put a television in your child's room. All the evidence shows this will undermine their reading skills.

Take it a step further: Sit down with your girl and together make a list of songs and shows that are inappropriate for her and discuss why. Let her make the list, so she herself can start identifying the negative influences. Then talk together about how having these things in her life only serves to harm her. "Told you so" or "I just don't like it" are not appropriate responses.

9

Don't Let Her Be the Only

The same thoughtful introspection that you give to television shows, friends, and the media must also be given to your parenting practice, because the actions you take can also negatively impact your children. One way to safeguard against this is by maintaining relationships with people who understand you and will help you feel connected.

Being connected to others can be emotionally, socially, and economically rewarding. But achieving and maintaining social connections can be difficult for trailblazing girls and women. The process of trailblazing can dislocate or interrupt connections as those who are forging new paths may find themselves on a journey without roadmaps. Yet, being socially connected remains vital for joyfulness and change-making. Reconciling these conflicting ideas (being the singular one and being connected to others) is one of many difficult charges for you, the caregiver.

For the most part, I have enjoyed being a trailblazer. I am the first in my family to go to college in the United States, I am the first and, so far, the only member of my family to be invited to the White House (under President Obama), and the first to found a nonprofit organization. I'm the only one to join the military. Also, I was the first among my close girlfriends to get married and have a child. Being the first can feel good, but at the same time, it can exact an emotional toll. And I have learned firsthand that the negative impact can intensify if you remain the only.

I could go on about the elation of opening new doors. Trailblazers certainly reap the rewards of breaking through visible or invisible barriers—the feeling of accomplishment and defying the odds is invigorating. But I must offer a cautionary tale. Given that the purpose of this book is to offer strategies for raising community-centered and socially connected girls, you can assume that I oppose any situation or effort that might fracture girls' ability to be socially and emotionally integrated, and I certainly balk at things that might impair their capacity to develop supportive communities.

My caution comes from knowing that trailblazers can fall prey to misguided beliefs of exceptionalism, a mistaken notion that they are above, different, or better than others. This belief can misalign, disrupt, or impede their connection with others. Furthermore, consistent praise of uniqueness and special talents can create an inflated sense of self-esteem.

Trailblazers, often highly intelligent and capable people, can also end up feeling like imposters. By its very design, being the only is isolating. You are often the singular person in a classroom, in a workplace, or on a field. There is no other person like you in sight. You might feel out of place, as if you don't truly belong. Ironically, people with imposter syndrome often feel like they are not as capable as others perceive them to be. They fight self-doubt by being overly critical, overpreparing, and overworking. From the outside, these actions look like ambition, but such drive can be unhealthy. Though feelings of imposter syndrome may seem like an individual issue, the real culprits are structures that are designed to foster and value homogeneity over diversity. The architects of these spaces are choosing to select only one person at a time and thereby fostering this feeling of isolation.

Now, I'm not trying to destroy the hopes and dreams we hold for our girls, any of whom might become the first woman president or the first woman to discover a cure for cancer. But, there are hazards to putting a girl in spaces where she is the only, and where she remains the only for extended periods of time. In such situations, our girls may become entitled or, worse, insecure—both dangerous and antithetical qualities to the development of joyful, change-making girls.

Entitlement and insecurity are particularly obstructive because they represent an absence of social and emotional connection to others. Entitlement can lead to being detached from others due to feelings of superiority, while insecurity can lead to isolation due to feelings of inferiority. Therefore, we must carefully weigh the challenges associated with the decision to *make* a girl a trailblazer. Consider the implications of keeping her in places that may breed social divisions. I use the word *make* purposefully here, because when a child is under ten years old, we adult caregivers have tremendous control over what she does. We decide where she will attend school, take dance classes, learn the piano, be tutored, play sports, and perform all her other activities. As we orchestrate her life, we must consider if she will be the first girl of her kind, and how that will shape her feelings about herself and others.

There will be times when the challenges of being the only may outweigh the benefits. I am aware of the guiding logic for many of us who move to communities and/or take jobs where we are the only—we envision that our presence and the contributions we make will change the culture and alter the structure for those who come after us. For example, being the only woman among senior staff at the workplace, or being the only person of color on the board of trustees at our children's school can be challenging. We believe that the personal sacrifices we are making will be for the greater good.

However, the cumulative research contradicts our altruistic assumptions. More often than not, our sacrifices will be for naught, and, worse, may take a toll on personal health. Research on women and work shows that, in an effort to demonstrate their competency, women work more hours than men—and the result is impaired physical health. Moreover, women are often fighting social isolation, performance pressures, sexual harassment, obstacles to mobility, and moments of both high visibility and invisibility, as well as co-workers' doubts about their competence and low levels of work-place social support. Chronic exposure to these stressors can make one vulnerable to disease. In fact, top female executives have higher rates of chronic disease than their male peers. Researchers from the University of Ohio found that women whose workweeks averaged sixty hours or more over three decades have higher rates of heart disease, cancer (excepting skin cancer), arthritis or rheumatism, diabetes or high blood sugar, chronic lung disease including bronchitis or emphysema, asthma, depression, and high blood pressure than those who worked fewer hours.

Beyond physical harm, being the only can lead to adoption of the very values that you seek to undermine. You see, when isolated, the only often seeks to facilitate large-scale organizational change. That's a noble goal, but systemic change requires more power than the only usually has. In the absence of a powerful change-making group to ally with, the only often relies on the support of those who currently have power. Indeed, studies conducted on women who are in these positions found that hopeful change-makers who turn to those in power to rectify inequality more often than not end up reinforcing the status quo and adopting distorted values themselves. The same power that led to the underlying underrepresentation ends up repeating itself, often in a new form, thereby making it unlikely that systematic change will occur. The only runs the risk of unconsciously drinking the dominant oppressive system's Kool-Aid or, worse, being beaten down by social isolation.

At this point you must be asking: How can I be all about creating change-making girls yet be against trailblazing? If trailblazing can harm us emotionally and spiritually, what must it be like for our girls? How can we advocate for trailblazing? Let me say emphatically that I am not against girls being the first in any arena. I just don't want to romanticize what that means. Instead, we should evaluate the risks and rewards with clarity and develop strategies that ultimately protect our girls. In other words, avoidance of trailblazing is not the answer; rather, awareness of the collateral effects is necessary, particularly if we consider putting our girls in spaces where they are the only.

Take the case of GrassROOTS SuperCamper Amina. Until she was eight, Amina was an only—the only Black girl in her ballet class, in her math group, indeed in every extracurricular activity in which her mother placed her. Her mom, Lisa, meant well. She would research "the best" ballet school, math group, or swimming class in their neighborhood and enroll Amina. Unfortunately, in their predominantly white suburb, the best usually meant no one else in the group looked like her daughter. Amina felt different, inadequate, and sad in these rooms. The more she internalized messages about who belonged (and who did not) in these so-called best spaces, the more she struggled to reconcile her own entitlement with the sense of being the other. She confessed that she wished her skin were lighter, her hair straighter, and her body shaped a different way.

As Lisa became more aware of the toll these predominantly white spaces were taking on her child, she began to put Amina in more racially mixed contexts, as well as in rooms where everyone's skin, hair, and body shape resembled those of her child. Not surprisingly, Amina began to shine because, finally, there were mirrors all around her, reflecting her beauty and light.

I faced a similar situation when Marley wanted to take gymnastics classes. Scheduling was difficult, as we had only a small window of time after school. Building a case for my tenure, I needed to spend my evenings reading or writing. I also wanted Marley to have plenty of downtime so we wouldn't have the cramped, rushed evenings that so many families had. We found a class in the nearby suburb of Livingston.

I was cautious because I knew the town was overwhelmingly white and affluent, lacking the economic and racial diversity of our town. Nevertheless, I went to the gymnastics class open house. The teachers were approachable, the facility clean, and the area very open. I came away excited for Marley to join. I was not concerned about whether she would feel comfortable. But I was concerned about the micro-exchanges about hair and body that might result from the lack of racial diversity among the participants and the staff. And so I asked two other mothers of Black daughters if their girls might also be interested in gymnastics. Fortunately, they were—but they had no way of getting their children to the class, and one mother was concerned about the cost of the tuition. After much thought, I agreed to transport all three children, and I offered to subsidize the tuition. Protecting my girl's positive feelings about her identity was worth the time and the money. For me this was a great return on investment. It was my workaround to prevent my child from being the only. Creating a microcosm of a community and supporting her with companions, so that they forged into new territory together, turned this potentially isolating only experience into a partnership. And it was a wonderful reminder that connection can be a powerful remedy for the pitfalls that threaten to derail trailblazers. Not all families will have the resources to do as I did, but you can be imaginative with the resources you do have.

As caregivers, we must watchfully guard against people who oppress and devalue women and girls. But we are often looking for obvious signs of this devaluation and can miss subtler cues. And the sly ones are just as dangerous. Idealism can blind us as we push our girls into boy-dominated spaces with the misguided belief that their presence will educate others or make the space more girl-friendly. A major challenge is that the pervasiveness of masculinity and the oppressiveness of the patriarchy are not always apparent, given how saturated our society is by the notion that men and boys are better than women and girls. Therefore, it is critical that we make these pernicious ideas clear to girls before throwing them into these spaces.

Furthermore, we know that spaces that are not intentional about including girls are often havens for gender inequity. Michael Kimmel, a professor of sociology at the State University of New York at Stony Brook, asserts that gender imbalances are often invisible to men and boys, such that they cannot see the ways in which gender inequity operates. They take for granted the ubiquitous examples of their power and dominance, remaining blind to their privileged social position. Too often, men and boys are like the fish in this Chinese proverb: Fish are the last to discover the ocean.

Of course, parents' lack of awareness of the inequities doesn't alter the reality that girls can be harmed by being the only in boy-dominated spaces. For example, girls often have to overdemonstrate their capacity, which can engender feelings of exceptionalism or, worse, may result in the girls being seen as just one of the boys. While this may not be initially viewed as a problem, it can lead to a lack of appreciation for the unique contribution of the girls. It can also result in the girls unwittingly accepting and sustaining the status quo of unjust standards. Further, the girl who succeeds in breaking the barrier may reject wanting more or even different types of girls to share her space because she may perceive that other girls may not rise to the occasion, and their failure will reflect poorly on her.

Breaking through the glass ceiling is often a goal for trailblazers. This pressure to transform exclusive spaces can be a double-edged sword. Girls who fracture the glass ceiling must guard against the accumulated insults that arise from the everyday experience of being treated as a second-class citizen. Scholars who study inequity find that repetitive negative treatment, especially through assaults so minor or subversive that they cannot be easily challenged, can cause quiet, lasting injury. One way the damage shows up is through feelings of not belonging. This is particularly true for those who are considered tokens.

Tokens, a term used since 1975, refers to individuals with marginal status; they have been permitted entrance to a social space, but have *not* been granted full rights of participation. When girls are perceived as tokens, it increases the odds that they will experience discrimination based on negative perceptions of their skills, authority, and leadership abilities, which in turn increases the likelihood that they will suffer psychological injury. Anticipating negative treatment and the accompanying chronic stress involved in continually maintaining a vigilant state is emotionally and physically detrimental. Sadly, many women and girls internalize this mistreatment as their own fault.

Studies of tokenism have found that this internalization leads to low self-esteem and depressive symptoms. Researchers at George

Mason University found that tokens experience enhanced visibility and increased performance pressure. They can also struggle with imposter syndrome, the nagging feeling that, despite their successes, they are actually not very good at what they do, and that sooner or later, someone, or everyone, will find out. According to some thirty years of research by psychologists, sociologists, and linguists, imposter syndrome affects women far more than men.

We faced the token issue when Marley was in third grade and wanted to play football. Her father had done a fine job of teaching her the sport. A fan of the Patriots franchise, she knew the names of NFL players and their positions on the field. Now Marley wanted to try out for her school's football team. When the school told her that girls "don't play football," Scott was appalled. He had never necessarily thought of himself as a feminist, but nothing makes a man a greater advocate for women than realizing that his wife will not have any more children and the one child he has is a girl. We protested with the league, and the situation was easily solved. It was a minor battle. We simply told them that she would play, and since their own rules never stated that girls could not play, Marley was allowed to play with the boys. In fact, she was chosen to be quarterback. Immediately, I began thinking about how to ensure that she wouldn't unwittingly embrace patriarchal ideas about boys' and girls' athletic competence. We thought we could forestall these problems by getting other girls to join the team, as we had done with gymnastics, but no other girls were interested. Instead, Scott became a coach for the team so he could keep a watchful eye on our daughter.

She played one season, and then decided that she didn't want to play anymore because it wasn't that fun. The boys didn't want to share the ball with her, and they wouldn't take her direction even though she knew the game as well or better than they did. She also didn't like that no girls were on the team. Instead, all the girls she knew, even the athletic ones, were cheerleaders. When I look back now, I'm not sure whether Marley's season on the football team was a net positive. I worry about the effect of her watching her friends cheer while she played. I am concerned about how she ended up characterizing boys and their ability (or lack of ability) to let girls lead. But, like most endeavors in parenting, time will tell what she ultimately takes away from this experience.

The enduring lesson is that as special as it might feel to be the first or the only, we must teach our girls that true success should not lead to further isolation. Instead, individual success should be healing. We gain a lot from trailblazing, but trailblazing alone will not restructure the environments we wish to change. We need allies and cohorts of similarly minded people. We need community.

Community is not defined by race, gender, or economic circumstance, but by a sense of being connected to others and having a common cause to support one another. Studies show that girls who feel grounded in a communal identity are more confident, engage in sexual activity at a later age, and have stronger self-efficacy throughout their lives than those who lack community. This applies to girls of all backgrounds. In contrast, the stress of isolation is one of the surest predictors of poor health. Therefore, we must encourage our girls to reach for the stars, but to find others to join them on the mission, so they can support one another along the way. Individual achievements are important, but an even greater achievement is when we all succeed.

ASSIGNMENTS

Prepare your child to be an only.

Make it clear to your girl why you have chosen an only space for her.
Explain to her your rationale so that she can better understand your reasons, as well as any reasons you may have for concern.

Without knowing your reasoning, she may have her own interpretations, which may be different from your reasons. As she becomes more articulate about her own feelings, ask her to share her excitements and concerns about the only space into which she is entering.

Learn more about the space in which you are putting her.
Before putting your girl into spaces where she is the only, investigate why no other girl or no other person of her ethnicity occupies that space. If the answer you get is, "They can't handle it," or "They're not ready," or "We haven't found a girl like you," then run. These responses suggest a blatant hostility toward girls. Find a different space in which to meet your girl's needs, desires, or goals.

What to do once she is in an only space
Make impromptu visits to the only space. Look out for disparities in how your girl is being treated. Observe what is asked of your girl compared to what is asked of others. Again, you want to make note that she is not being ostracized (not being included in activities) or exotified (treated as overly exceptional such that she is not able to be viewed as a community member).

Check in with your girl regularly to ensure that she's not absorbing any girl-bashing ideas or falling prey to negative self-talk.
Pay attention to what she says, the words she uses. Without criticizing her, engage in conversation around these ideas and help her identify their source and recognize how they are misguided. Be on the lookout for language that generalizes or diminishes the abilities of girls. Look out for girl-bashing phrases like "Girls just can't do what boys do," "Boys are just better at this than girls," or "Girls will cry if they lose."

Thriving while in only spaces

Teach her how to build a supportive community around herself.

Supportive networks reduce isolation and increase well-being. Though you and she may have a mission to expand a space, that often takes time. In the interim, she will want and need to succeed. Having a network of friends can buffer the challenges she faces in only spaces. Help your girl understand that success in life relies on being connected to others. Here is one process:

1. Using the list of qualities of a good friend that you developed on page 114, help her create a profile of her ideal group of friends. Include as many details and characteristics as possible.
2. Have her identify qualities that she needs to develop within herself. Remember that like attracts like. Help your girl understand that if she wants a friend who is adventurous, she too will need to be a risk-taker. If she would like a friend who is creative, she must be willing to showcase her imagination. The more you focus on developing the qualities that are important to her and you, the better the chances are of attracting a friend who shares your values and goals.

Cultivating an environment of allies

Though your girl may be the only in the class or on the field, she will need peers. Those persons may look different from your girl, have different skills and talents, and act differently. She must be taught that despite these differences she must seek to become an ally and make an ally. Your job as caregiver is to provide her with an operative definition of an ally. An ally is someone who stands with or advocates for individuals and groups other than their own. In her case, an ally is the person who might ask people to stop girl bashing. For example, an ally might say, "Stop that; that is not true" or "We should not say mean things about girls." Allies often highlight and elevate diverse perspectives and people. Also, allies will ask questions about what and who are missing. For example, an ally might ask, "Why aren't there more girls on the team?" or "Why aren't we assigned more diverse books in our class?" Similar to friends, allies reduce social isolation and help girls feel safe. Once girls feel safe, they are safe to be themselves, and they can thrive.

Help her understand and treat people like valuable resources.

Ask her to tell you a story of a recent achievement. Together, identify the people she needed to make the success possible. She can name the specific type of support she received, whether emotional or instrumental (practical). Through these conversations she may begin to take stock of the ways these individuals provided her with a valuable set of resources and how those resources were critical to her ability to succeed. Once she has completed this first part, ask her to identify her role in helping others succeed. She needs to be able to see the reciprocal nature of friendships. Whatever she desires in friends and allies, she must embody that herself.

10

Build Her a Safety Net

Like the basic needs—food, clothing, shelter—our social and emotional needs significantly influence our cognition and our behavior. For those of us seeking to parent like it matters, this means paying careful attention to our own needs and those of our girls. It means building them a safety net, as well as ensuring and providing for their physical safety, including putting a roof over their heads, saving for their education, clothing them appropriately, and providing their meals. Unfortunately, for many of us, ensuring that we provide a safety net for our children usually translates into a myopic focus on financial security. But the evidence is clear: Safety is more than supplying external material resources. Girls need emotional safety as well. A girl who has an emotional safety net will dare anything. She will feel unabashed, free, and adventurous.

These feelings are critical because in our society so much of being a girl or a woman is about constraint—constraining our bodies as well as our thoughts, even our ideas. For girls of color like my daughter, who are often asked to shrink into the background, we have to be intentional about making sure our children feel safe to express exactly who they are.

There are several components to building an emotional safety net for your girl. The first is establishing a loving community. We must consciously surround our girls with people who are invested in their healthy development—people they can talk to and go to for advice. That network of folks may change over time, so evaluating whether your girl is emotionally centered is a constantly evolving process of trial and error.

In my experience, some parents focus so keenly on providing for their children's basic needs that they do not devote enough energy to their own or to their girls' emotional needs. Unfortunately, this focus can contribute to tunnel vision. I have witnessed how this type of single-minded attention on financial needs can handicap girls' emotional well-being.

Parents find their way to our program, excited to be a part of the training experience themselves, and also drawn to the breadth of our curriculum. But some households provide a stronger emotional foundation for their children than others. It's not necessarily the fault of the parents, but things like divorce, addiction, previous poverty experience, and other life stressors shape parenting practices, and sometimes those concerns create a series of actions that can leave a girl vulnerable in ways that even her parents don't realize. While parents are eager to shore up girls' educational and social supports, they can miss her emotional distress and needs. The result is that sometimes we have SuperGirls who are frequently late or who come unprepared to camp—missing out on some of their favorite activities and opportunities to connect with other girls. Some girls also have emotional mood swings, expressing happiness and being engaged in some moments, then becoming melancholy and filled with despair in the next.

Girls will present themselves as well-adjusted even when they are in an emotionally capricious place; they push themselves to show appreciation for their parents' efforts, yet want so much more. At SuperCamp our role is to alert caregivers to the gaps in their safety net and help them fill these holes. Through conversations with parents, we help them discover when their girls are feeling unseen. Despite parents' labor to provide for their children's physical needs, girls' emotional needs frequently go unmet. Luckily, once we are all on the same page and can identify together what is contributing to a girl's emotional state, the GrassROOTS team can support parents in figuring out how to expand their daughters' worlds and build greater levels of social and emotional support.

Given the demands of their jobs, some parents feel like they simply cannot allocate as much time to their children's emotional needs as they can to their physical ones. It's easy to check off the list of back-to-school shopping and make sure the girl is signed up for the right afterschool activities, but it's harder to set aside the time to sit with a child to talk about her feelings, especially her anxieties and fears. Emotional desires are sometimes cast as extras, and as a result, girls are often trained to adjust to situations and to deprioritize their emotional needs. This false framing is commonplace in parenting; many of us struggle to balance these seemingly competing needs of financial responsibility and emotional well-being. This struggle reveals a flaw in traditional conceptualizations of the safety net.

Our work with families facing these challenges involves attending to three core issues: reducing the SuperGirl's social isolation, building her emotional resilience and honesty, and enhancing her caregivers' awareness of how their actions and inactions impact her emotionally. To support her caregivers' awareness, we request that caregivers participate in weekly individual sessions with the team therapist. To help the SuperGirls build their emotional resiliency, we sometimes increase the number of times she sees the therapist during program time. And to reduce the girl's feelings of social isolation, we encourage her caregivers to let her stay late after camp and hang out on the weekend with other SuperGirls. Finally, we help girls express their feelings by helping them increase their vocabulary—which means building basic literacy. We understand the relationship between reading and emotional expression; as a girl's literacy increases, so does her ability to express her feelings. But not all girls love to read. Therefore, we design our program to enhance girls' overall literacy. Luckily, each year we have educators who volunteer with our program who help our girls become more literate. By the last week of camp, girls are better able to express themselves with an increased, more sophisticated vocabulary—and a newfound excitement about reading.

We have seen that reading opens up a child's spirit. Improved literacy enhances girls' ability to express themselves and communicate their innermost thoughts, in ways that allow their parents to hear them in new ways. Parents are sometimes overwhelmed by this new information, but the family therapist is there to help them integrate it. As a result, we have seen parents change their work schedules and take days off to spend more time with their children, and we've seen the girls thrive with this newfound attention.

The preoccupation with financial safety concerns can sometimes overshadow the need for our girls' emotional safety. I know this well. Scott and I have had meager incomes most of our adult lives, and we have been concerned about many of these same safety concerns. However, from the onset I have prioritized Marley's emotional safety, because I struggled in my youth to feel seen and heard.

Emotional safety must be buttressed with physical safety. In our own home, Scott and I are equal-ish partners in creating a secure life for Marley. Indeed, when she was little, we called Scott the "safety officer," because he was exceedingly vigilant about her safety. He would let her play and jump, but never too much, for fear she would get hurt. In contrast, I refused to childproof our apartment, insisting it was far simpler if we just didn't own furniture that could harm her, which meant no glass tables or pieces with sharp edges, and putting household items like knives, pills, and bleach in high cabinets beyond her reach. When it came to the stairs, I thought we could just teach her how to climb them so she wouldn't fall. I believe that kids are fully capable of learning appropriate and healthy behaviors if we teach them early and we explain and demonstrate precautions. Many of life's lessons come through trial and error.

Looking back now, I laugh, and I feel grateful for having a partner who was willing to work with me, despite his misgivings. We shared the ultimate goal of protecting our daughter, and Scott's support allowed me to be the parent I wished to be while allowing Marley to feel the security she needed to thrive.

If Marley's physical safety has been overseen mostly by her dad, her emotional safety has largely been my job. I don't mean to understate Scott's contribution in this area; it is simply that we concern ourselves with differing aspects of her safety and have differing strategies about how to keep her safe. He is happy to keep Marley's world small and filled primarily with family members. He has high stranger danger. People do wacky things, and his job as he sees it is to keep her far away from these wacky people and their ways. I agree with him generally. However, as people do indeed do wacky things, I believe that as parents we must do several things: help our children identify which things are wacky, know and recognize wacky people, and if possible, help these people do fewer wacky things. Children will not live in the bubble of their houses forever, so we have to help them and help the world if we really are going to keep them safe. It's what I desire for all girls—a world that encompasses everything they can dream, yet within which they can feel safe. This is the focus of my academic research, my work at Grass-ROOTS, and, of course, my parenting style.

But I deeply value Scott's approach, because it links emotional and physical safety. His position recognizes that people who might physically harm us should never be trusted with our children's emotional safety. We must teach our girls to identify and stay clear of both physical and emotional dangers.

As Marley grew, Scott and I would point out problematic behaviors we saw in public, explaining to her why we were challenged by some of the things we saw. We also pointed out behaviors that reinforced our values. For example, the nanny or parent who sat on the phone with their backs to their children on the playground? Unsafe. The caregiver who did not correct the child who hit another child? Unsafe. The adult who thought it was funny when a group of kids laughed at someone who fell? Unsafe. The group of kids who refused to let a child play with them? Unsafe. In each of these instances, we explicitly, even loudly, explained to our daughter why such actions were unsafe—hoping the offenders would hear us and change their behavior. For us, the definition of unsafe was clear: any action that results in harming you physically or emotionally; people who say or do things that hurt others; places where someone feels excluded or demeaned.

We talk to our SuperGirls a lot about physical and emotional safety. Many complain about the things they hear boys say on the school bus. Some boys use sexually derogatory phrases like "hit that fat ass." Some call girls bitches; others will reveal personal and intimate information about girls. I have listened to reports from girls about being the last girl on the bus, concerned that boys might say those things to them. Other girls are worried about dark hallways at school or the catcalling that happens when they are walking on the street. Girls often come to camp being very informed about strategies to stay physically safe, but rarely do they report having conversations with their parents about how to stay emotionally safe.

At SuperCamp we talk a lot about emotional safety, which relies on trust and reliability. We talk to our girls and their families about the importance of taking time to know each other so that they can learn to trust each other. Building this trust demands that they are true to their word and honest about their feelings. It is also important that they recognize that trust is gradual. Trust increases and improves over time if people are consistent.

Here's another thing—and you aren't going to be surprised to hear me say it—safety is *essential* to joyfulness. I urge you to create a world filled with a group of people around your girl who allow her to feel young, curious, and fun loving; a world that values her childhood, encourages her mistakes, and supports her full self; a world in which each area of her life has been deliberately and lovingly constructed, and in which the rules governing each developmental stage are clearly understood and practiced—a world where she feels safe, emotionally and physically.

One way to achieve that is by being consistent. Providing consistency in her daily routines, particularly in the places she goes and the people she hangs out with, will help her feel safe. Research on routines shows that repeated engagement in familiar spaces both provides a predictable structure that guides behavior and offers an emotional climate that supports children's early development. Emotional connections established in these ritualized settings facilitate relationship satisfaction and increase children's socioemotional functioning. Routines provide a context for children to practice emerging skills and afford them an opportunity to connect with the adults who organize the world.

Build your girl's sense of safety and stability through routines by putting her in familiar environments. At GrassROOTS, I use routines to assist girls in knowing what will happen next. We review the day's schedule after community circle. All girls are asked to wear watches to camp so that they can be aware of the time. We also build in transition time between activities when older girls help younger girls put their things away, prepare to go to the bathroom, and wash their hands.

For Marley, we used places that we frequent, like bookstores and diners, to build this infrastructure around her. People and places served as protective armors. When we moved to Ann Arbor, Marley was four months old, and we knew practically no one. After spending several months learning the community we found a Borders, a great bookstore near campus. Every Thursday, at the end of my workday, I would pick Marley up from daycare, and we would visit the bookstore. The quiet, cozy kid section was perfect for us. The space was beautifully decorated with soft mats and bright colors that made for a stimulating environment. Marley would crawl over to the bookshelves and choose six books to "read" to me, and I would choose six to read to her. She would sit on my lap, open a book, and pretend to read to me. I would listen attentively. After she was done with her book, I read to her from one of the books I had selected. We did this for about an hour, or until we felt like it was time to go.

Sometimes Scott joined us and then we grabbed dinner after. Scott is not an avid reader of storybooks, but he reads several newspapers daily and voraciously consumes literature on hip-hop, sneakers, mechanics, and history. He will read anything about how and where things are made. He loves any and all machines, from trucks to drills, and he scares me with his knowledge of American and European wars and the weapons used in these disputes. My husband is exceptionally brilliant. On the days he joined us, he would find magazines he liked and share them with Marley. She sat in his lap as he combed over the pages. I would eventually have to pull him away and back to the kid section. Reading was so much more fun with him because he is a master of making animal sounds. The best is his elephant noise. To this day, when he makes this noise we all laugh out loud.

Going to the bookstore consistently was initially about filling time before heading home, but it evolved into a way to make public spaces safe for Marley. The more the people who worked in Borders saw us, the more we became a part of the store's community culture. When we first started going, I would not allow Marley to roam very far; like all new moms I was hypervigilant. She couldn't talk, and so she had to stay within an arm's length of me. As she grew and became more verbal, I allowed her to explore a bit more, knowing that whenever she was not in sight, the people in the store knew she belonged to me. Of course, I had spoken to and assessed the people who worked in the store and judged that none seemed to pose a physical threat to my child's well-being. We also had the same salesperson help us from week to week. The sheer consistency of our engagement made the bookstore space feel safe.

When we moved to New Jersey, Marley was almost three years old. We retained this practice of going to Borders in East Hanover, a few miles from our house. For six years, until the bookstore, sadly, went out of business, we kept up our Thursday bookstore visits. The salespeople in New Jersey, once again, became familiar with my daughter and knew our routine. After ordering a warm vanilla soy milk and a brownie for Marley and a caramel macchiato with skim milk and banana for me, I would find a spot in the children's section. Marley would choose her six books, I would choose my six books, and we would read them together. Marley was also allowed to choose one book to buy every week. We agreed that the cost of the book had to begin with a number that was the same as her age or lower. So at age five she could buy a book that cost up to $5.99, at age six $6.99, and so on.

When she got to be eight years old, her reading level jumped, and so did the cost of the books she now wanted. The books she was interested in cost $12.99 and up, making our tradition more expensive. Sure, we also had the library, but the bookstore had more new books, plus they had the café with those delicious beverages. We decided as a family to increase the budget for Marley's book choices, and we continued the tradition until she was almost ten years old. By the time the Borders in our community was set to close, the staff all knew Marley by name and gave her parting treats. She had grown up in front of them, and she had felt free and safe there. We even held playdates at the bookstore, allowing Marley and her friends free rein to explore the aisles independent of grownups.

Another safe space we created was our local diner. We had breakfast there once a week from the time Marley was five. When we started eating there, I would go to the bathroom with Marley to make sure that she was safe. If she and her dad got there before me, she was not allowed to go to the bathroom until I arrived. She could not be out of our sight for one second. We had selected this breakfast spot because it was seldom crowded and the staff was friendly. We committed to this place as "our diner," and even when it became more popular, we stuck to our routine. We sat in roughly the same seats, always had the same waiter, and ordered the same things. Over time—a year or two, the cashier and other staff came to know us, which allowed us to give Marley more autonomy. We could sit at our table while Marley went to the bathroom by herself. Marley's freedom in that diner didn't come about simply because she was getting older—though that mattered—but it was aided by the fact that the space felt familiar and predictable. Though people sometimes call us boring because we keep going to the same places, we value being around people who create an environment in which our daughter can feel free.

While space matters for safety, so does clear and consistent communication. At the New Jersey Borders, when she was about seven years old we began by letting Marley roam around the children's section on her own for five minutes. What she didn't know was that Scott and I would surveil her surreptitiously from a distance. We taught her how to tell time in kindergarten and bought her a watch so that she could keep track of how long she was "on her own." As she became more responsible, her time away from us grew to fifteen minutes. When she got to about ten years old, she was allowed to leave the children's section and be away from us in the bookstore for thirty minutes, if she was with a friend. By this time, she was in sixth grade and had a phone, and could text us the location where we would meet up with her and her friends.

Marley is a teenager now, and she is free to be in the mall by herself for up to two hours, as long as she checks in every hour. She can go to the bathroom by herself at airports, and I can leave her in the bookstore while I get my lashes done or my shopping completed. Marley has learned to be aware of her surroundings, and she is a skilled and reliable communicator. She texts us throughout the day to let us know how her day is going, and when she gets off the school bus, she calls one of us to say that she is home. She understands the value of communication and its role in keeping her safe, and her willing accountability has made our jobs infinitely easier.

There is another kind of safe space that we must carve out for a girl—a place in which she can fail spectacularly. Mistakes always feel worse when we make them in front of strangers, and we never want our girls to think, "Oh my God, I can never do that again!" For our daughter, who has an expanded public presence since her social campaign took off, we have countered this possibility by deliberately reducing her immediate circle to a core group of people who genuinely love and support her. We want people around her who have taken the time to know her and are invested in her healthy development. They are friends of all ages who Marley can talk with freely and turn to for advice; she is safe to be herself among them.

With this loving and loyal circle around her, if Marley takes a risk and falters, she will have supportive voices in her ear, encouraging her to try again. It is critically important to us that nothing feels too dire for her. And as she moves deeper into her teenage years, we want her to be at liberty to be moody and complicated without being sullen and pessimistic. We want her to continue being an adventurer, because that will offer her ample opportunities to learn to regulate the emotional part of failing. Later in life, when the stakes get higher, we hope she will have developed the psychological agility to manage difficult situations.

At SuperCamp and in our home, we have developed a set of criteria for how to identify an emotionally safe person. The first attribute they must have is kindness. We encourage parents to seek out and invite in people who are generous toward their children, people who see and value the less visible aspects of who their daughter is—not just those who offer compliments about her physical self or her intellect. The next attribute is generosity. Emotionally safe people are willing to share information about themselves; they are not guarded about themselves and their own mistakes. We find that generous people are often emotionally responsive to children. Finally, we look for people who are expressive with words but also good listeners. They take the time to hear children's ideas before asserting their own.

Because our daughter has excelled in many things, people sometimes think they have to cut us down as parents or undermine her achievements. A major part of our daughter's safety net is making sure she is surrounded by people who treat her the way we would treat her, being honest and considerate yet not overly indulgent, and definitely not demeaning. And we rejoice when people are willing to teach our daughter something new.

Today, Marley's safety circle is filled with folks who are optimistic and fun, people who can be trusted to be sensitive to our daughter's thoughts and desires. It is also important to me that she is surrounded by people who can safely demonstrate physical affection for her, because we know that safe touching can help children recognize and validate their own emotions.

Helping girls choose a circle of people who are emotionally safe can be challenging as our communities constantly evolve with school changes, home relocations, families rearranging themselves, and people coming in and out of our lives under various circumstances. The circle might contain that committed friend who will call when you are not feeling well and offer to watch your child for the day so you can get some rest. It's important to observe your friends with your girl, though, as an emotionally unsafe person might not be apparent to you until he or she yells at your child for making a simple mistake.

Perhaps you're thinking: Isn't an extended family a ready-made safety net? Well, not necessarily. Selecting the people in your safety net is not always as simple as looking to family members.

A third of the parents in GrassROOTS are single moms. They often share stories of caution and triumph. One of them, I'll call her Veronica, told me her story of her daughter and ex-husband. She experienced a painful divorce from her daughter's father after he cheated on her during pregnancy. Despite this unexpected family formation, she was determined that her little girl, I'll call her Kelly, should have a "complete family." Veronica's use of that phrase told me she saw herself and her daughter as an incomplete family.

She had this view in large part because on more than one occasion, Kelly's father failed to show up when he said he would. When Kelly stayed at his home twice a month, per her parents' agreement, Kelly reported to her mother that her father consistently berated her, undermining her ideas, commenting on how she looked, and criticizing the things she liked. To him, Kelly couldn't seem to do anything right. She told her mother about it, but her mother insisted that was just the way he was. She followed their arranged agreement and continued to send Kelly to stay with her father. During one visit, Kelly's dad slapped her across the cheek because she refused to eat her vegetables at dinner. He then warned her not to tell her mother. Fortunately, Kelly did not heed his instruction. Instead she found a phone, locked herself in the bathroom, and tearfully called her mom, telling her what had happened and asking her to please come and get her. When Veronica sent Kelly back to her dad's house two weekends later, I became really concerned. Veronica wanted Kelly's father in her life so much so that, by allowing her father's abusive presence, she was neglecting her daughter's need for a safe and loving space in which to grow. Veronica explained that her own father had not been present in her life, and she had always longed to know him. I sympathized, of course—but I gingerly expressed my worry.

Veronica and I had several intense conversations about her situation and the damage that forced exposure to her ex-husband might be doing to her child. Veronica was in an untenable situation; she wanted to do what she believed would be in the long-term interests of her child, and all the master messages suggest that two parents are always better than one. Luckily, through our conversations, Veronica found a new way. A biological father isn't the only adult man who can teach a girl how loving, caring men behave. Veronica began to think about all the positive men in Kelly's life, including the supportive fathers who were part of the GrassROOTS community. At last she asked Kelly the one question she had never thought to put to her: Did she want to keep spending time with her father? Kelly's response was an unequivocal *no*. Stunned by how emphatic her daughter was when given the choice, Veronica at last realized that Kelly wasn't pining for her father. Rather, the decision to send Kelly back to her dad was influenced by the fact that Veronica was still pining for her own dad. She realized she had fallen into the classic trap of trying to give her child what she herself had never had, meanwhile missing what her daughter actually needed. Despite her best intentions, Veronica was not parenting from a *joyful* place.

Cumulative social science research shows that fathers play a significant role in their children's lives and that this relationship is among the most important factors influencing a child's psychological adjustment. But while fathers clearly matter, as Michael Lamb, a Cambridge psychologist, wrote in 2010, "We think it is misguided to see increased paternal involvement as a universally desirable goal." What matters more, he argues, is not whether caregivers are biologically related to the children, but that caregivers are positive adults in low-conflict unions who are invested in promoting the children's well-being through age-appropriate monitoring of their activities, as well as warm and supportive disciplinary strategies.

If, in fact, it becomes clear that it's better for your girl to be parented solo, then you will need to get creative, finding a trusted second adult who can step in when you need a break from driving the parenting train. Having a supportive community of family members, in-laws, caring friends, and fellow parents will allow you to realize the resources you need to become the loving and intentional caregiver your girl needs—with or without the presence of the other half of the team responsible for her genetic code. If this seems daunting, don't worry. There are some exercises at the end of this chapter to help you figure out how to do this.

Ultimately, we want to prepare our girls to create their own safety nets. We want them to choose places where they feel physically and emotionally safe. As with so many aspects of raising them, the idea is to pass the torch of responsibility to them over the years, gradually, gently, so that the care you have poured into them can inspire them to pour the same care into themselves, making them ready to become change-makers.

ASSIGNMENTS

Establish a routine to create a safe space outside your home for your girl.

Your local bookstore, restaurant, or café are all good options. Get to know the people who work there. Find a favorite park or activity and fold it into your lives. Gradually, you can expand your child's borders, ensuring she understands the importance of staying in communication when she is out in the world. You will have to trust your gut and learn from her when the time is right to expand her borders.

Help your girl identify whom she can trust with her feelings.

Be honest in your assessment of the people around your girl. If you don't tell her what you think, she will assume that anyone you know can be trusted, not just with her physical safety, but also her emotional safety. Point out those people in your life who are sensitive to her emotions and who are invested in her ability to navigate within a healthy environment. These people will help her thrive.

Sitting down together, you and your girl should each get a

piece of paper. Fold the paper in half. On the left side of the paper write at the top "My Physical Safety List," and on the right side of the paper write "My Emotional Safety List." Ask your girl to write down the names of five people currently in her life who she feels look out for her physical safety. On your list, you should write down the names of five people currently in her life who you feel look out for her safety. Do not share answers yet. Repeat the process for the emotional safety list. Write down the names of five people who she feels look out for her emotional safety. People she can talk to about her feelings; people who will listen to her without harsh judgment; people who will support her desires for herself. You should also write down your list. Once you have completed your lists, compare and discuss who is listed and who is not listed and why.

If you both realize your lists are on the small side, this may be a sign to expand the circle. As you do so, intentionally seek out people who are warmly responsive, since they will be capable of helping your girl to understand, express, and modulate her thoughts, behaviors, and feelings through coaching and modeling safe and supportive interactions.

Make yourself a list of the supportive people in your parenting community.

Even when you are parenting with a partner, you can feel under-resourced and alone. Take stock of who is and has been around to help you parent. The list you create should include the people you feel you can call on at a moment's notice, as well as those who might not be available to pinch-hit on babysitting, but who are always ready to lend an ear and offer wise guidance. You may find that you have more and better resources than you realized.

Reach out to the people who are part of your village and say thank you.

Whether you call them, write them letters, or send texts, let them know how much you appreciate and rely on them. This will help them recognize the importance of their role in your—and your daughter's—life and will have the added bonus of making you feel less alone. One idea I love is to send them a biannual newsletter informing them about your girl, including big and small details.

Host a community parenting awards ceremony, where you give honors to the various members of your community for the ways they help you parent.

Make it a party and create fun categories (your daughter can help), such as "And the Parenting Support Award for Best Driver in a Pinch goes to . . ." With a healthy dose of laughter and comedy, you'll be letting people know how much they matter.

Part IV

Change-Maker

Since this chapter is probably what you came here for, I want to tell you at the start of this section what I tell all the first-time parents at GrassROOTS: If you want a joyful, change-making girl or you want to resurrect a seemingly dispassionate girl, you must lay the foundation for making that possible. You, yes, you, the parent, must become a change-maker yourself. If that point is not already clear to you, please let me make it even more lucid here. A joyful, change-making girl will not happen without a joyful, change-making parent.

Whether you are beginning the parenting journey or far down the road, there are several things you can do right now to make sure that your girl is joyful, remains joyful, and grows to become a change-maker. You can encourage her curiosity and awaken her imagination, teach her to value science, and help her develop a learning mindset. You can also create spaces so that she is comfortable having courageous conversations and feels safe expressing her opinions. This will mean that you must be willing to hear her voice. In addition to listening to her and valuing her unique perspectives, you must expose her to many things so that she can develop her interests and her own point of view. Finally, you can help her see that her interests and passions are the tools that she can use to make a positive difference in the world.

11

Encourage Her Curiosity and Awaken Her Imagination

If our ultimate goal is to raise joyful girls who have the will and heart to improve the world around them, then we must encourage their curiosity about that very world. This means cultivating in our girls an imagination that can envision change and create ways to implement these changes. Like you, girls need a learning mindset. For many of us, adulthood can be synonymous with the completion of learning, particularly if we didn't love our own school years. But parenting must be about learning—learning and knowing things about yourself, your girl, and the world around you.

You see, our job as caregivers is to create a world where our girls are always learning and always seeking to learn. You must model that process for them. Since we cannot count on formal educational training to always support this goal (if at all), we need to nurture a curious child by laying a rich soil for learning before she even starts school, fertilizing it with ideas and a love for fact-based information. Regardless of our own educational experience, we can help our girls become inquisitive about the world around them, starting from a very young age. The best way we can do this is by introducing them to facts and fostering creativity.

The future that we are seeking for our children demands that we embrace facts; we must be willing to consider facts that don't support our worldview or personal experiences. Today, too many of us falsely believe that our lives are the yardstick by which we can measure what is true. But the world is more complex, and facts can help us understand complex issues. Even more of us cannot discern what information is fact-based and what is opinion.

Valuing facts seems more and more difficult these days. In a report entitled "Facts Matter," Sarah Rosen Wartell of the Urban Institute argues that "facts matter more than ever in this time of polarization and potentially dramatic policy change." She poignantly asks, "What is the future of our civil society if we can't agree on basic facts?"

Evaluating the information we give our children, especially when we source from the Internet, is incredibly important. With more and more information available to us on the Internet, it can be tempting to treat all sources as though they're created equal. But an article on Wikipedia is *not* as reliable as one in *Scientific American*. As facts become more and more elusive in our current media landscape, it's vital that you provide a strong foundation for determining the validity of information you consume online—both for yourself *and* for your girl. If you're unsure where to start, don't worry. There are resources available for getting smart about misinformation on the Internet (see Resources, page 215).

While external fake news is an all-too-real threat, we must recognize that, too often, as parents we create our own fake news. We run away from or deny facts, choosing instead to make up narratives to explain social or scientific phenomena. We tell our children tall tales about where babies come from and why some people are poor or unhealthy.

We must remember that while the ugly truth of a fact can sometimes feel too harsh a pill to swallow, understanding factual information allows us to assess the root causes of the very social issues and phenomena we want to protect our children from; facts can even help us understand the differences that exist among us. But instead of arming our children with the truth, we opt for digestible lies. When facts are complex, we evade, misdirect, or misinform.

Now, before we go any further, I want to make one thing clear:

I'm not talking about Santa Claus, the Easter Bunny, or the Tooth Fairy. Though many parents struggle with whether or not to expose these mythical childhood figures, researchers like Alison Gopnik, professor of psychology at the University of California, Berkeley, agree that "young children have this ability to know that something is mythical, but yet experience it vividly at the same time." Said differently, it is safe to believe in the myth of Santa and others because children recognize that myths and fairy tales exist in different worlds than our day-to-day reality. However, it is not safe to deny the existence of known and agreed-upon social and scientific evidence. Children need to learn very early on that facts can help us overcome challenges and learn from our mistakes to develop relevant solutions.

Facts inform.

Facts help us get to the truth.

But what are facts?

Facts are pieces of information gathered through the scientific method, whereby information is heavily scrutinized to find and develop evidence of whether something is true. The process is rigorous and demands documented proof from diverse, vetted, unbiased sources. However, it is important to note that almost nothing can be proven with 100 percent certainty. Even as we accept facts, we should maintain a healthy dose of skepticism and be comfortable with ambiguity. Skepticism is healthy for your girl—it is a sign that she engages with facts and questions the status quo.

Okay, maybe at this point you're thinking, "I have to teach my kids facts? Isn't that what I send them to school for?" Yes and no. You see, children learn many facts at school, but that sense of inquisitiveness and imagination should not be confined singularly to formal educational spaces. It must be built everywhere, beginning at home.

Once you start looking for opportunities to foster an atmosphere of learning in the home, you will quickly realize that it makes everything fun. Scott and I have used every opportunity we can to teach Marley. We organized each day around a subject and created a schedule of activities that we posted in the kitchen. We never had a specific "study time" but simply incorporated learning into the daily routines of our lives. We looked for ways to create fun activities that would teach her about a topic we had in mind.

In the early days, we focused on literacy and providing her with as many words as possible to express herself. So, to teach her letters and expose her to the alphabet, I'd scatter ABC cards on the living room floor. Then I lined up the letters from A to E in the correct order until soon she was doing the same thing without my help. Using number cards, she and I competed to see who could crawl to the numbers 1 to 5 the fastest.

Science and math lessons often came in the form of playing or listening to music. After work, Scott would sit down at the piano keyboard with her and teach her the various notes. He would play a note and then she would follow. He taught her to create her own sounds using his sampler—an electronic musical instrument that uses sound recordings of real instrument sounds or excerpts from recorded songs. She learned rhythms (and the math behind them) from listening repeatedly to accessible, age-appropriate music—from the Wiggles to They Might Be Giants to the Isley Brothers.

Now, language and music might appear to be two fundamentally different skills, but experimental psychologists have found many commonalities in the psychological underpinnings of music and language. Scholars argue that behind the seemingly effortless perception of music, there exists a set of complex cognitive processes; we primarily learn these processes through repeated exposure to language and music. Additionally, functional imaging studies have found that music and language activate similar regions of the brain.

Music is also important because scientists have found strong correlation between music aptitude, rhythm achievement, and numeracy achievement. Listening to music, moving to music, making music, and singing enhance spatial skills, specifically our ability to see patterns. This skill set is particularly critical for social activists because it is the way social scientists are able to identify inequities. We examine social patterns to better understand whether injustices have occurred by chance or because of outside forces.

As Marley grew older, we introduced more scientific subjects to foster her curiosity. Scott taught her foundational concepts of physics and chemistry by setting up household experiments. They destroyed many T-shirts, used countless glue sticks, and messed up the kitchen more times than I can recall—all in the name of science. Scott holds a degree in Earth and Atmospheric Sciences and is a serious nature lover, so it was common for me to discover containers of dirt in the fridge next to the yogurt and raspberries. After school, I could find my little girl outside, fully dressed up, digging for worms to better understand how they moved, what they ate, and how long they could survive.

I share these examples of everyday learning experiences for Marley because I know that everyone's household is going to have different infrastructure that can support learning. However, I believe that any household *can* support learning, in its own way. Scott and I had limited family support and had to be creative with the talents we had, but the strategies we chose are hardly the only ways to encourage curiosity and a love of learning. What's important is that you choose an approach that works for your particular family and matches your skills and talents. The objective is to build routine activities into your daily learning that will increase your girl's foundational knowledge and general inquisitiveness about the world— the building blocks for raising a child who will reject bigotry, identify the hypocrisy in racism, advocate for others, challenge inequity, and work collectively to engender social activism.

One element I would recommend including in your approach, no matter what, is reading with your girl. Each night, without fail, from the day she was born, we read to Marley. We're not alone in this practice: It turns out that in American households, approximately 52% of young children are read to every day by a parent. That's a pretty good number, but not a *great* number. These daily reading routines are important for a child's early literacy development, and especially for their cognitive development and later reading skills. But as wonderful as the science on reading together is, we were less focused on its educational benefits and more on how much *fun* it was. Reading together was a family routine; it was our time together. For us, it was a way to share adventures, to travel in our imaginations together, and to share ideas. We would pause and ask Marley questions along the way. Even when she couldn't talk we would ask her which animal she liked best, and ask her to point to her favorite. Our questions progressed from simple identification (What is this?) to description questions (What color/shape/size is this?) to closed-ended questions (What is happening here?), ultimately progressing to open-ended and higher-order questions (What could be happening here?) as she got older. We tried to ensure she enjoyed the experience and saw reading as fun. We also felt that if she liked to read, she would eventually use these opportunities to share her opinions and would discover that books could deepen her sense of self as well as develop her vocabulary. But in the early years, we simply focused on making reading fun.

For us, fun meant that we needed variation. We always chose diverse books; some had characters that looked like her and some did not. It was important to us that she had both mirrors and windows to the world. She could see reflections of herself in books as well as observe and have access to other types of narratives.

Reading is also a wonderful way to foster *creativity* in your girl—the second tenet so crucial to creating inquisitive, joyful change-makers. We hear the word *creativity* a lot, but what does it really mean? Creative imagination is defined as the capacity to generate novel or unusual ideas. Researchers have established that early and extended exposure to television can negatively impact the imaginations of children and can stymie the creative ideas and play skills of preschoolers. Such impediments are disruptive because the imagination liberates us from the tyranny of our immediate circumstances, allowing us to conceive of alternative possibilities and explore a range of potential futures and conditions. The imagination allows our girls to test out ideas in their heads and to consider things, even those that may not seem practical. It allows them to role-play and enact various experiences they may have had or something that interests them. Heavy television, on the other hand, robs children of these skills by pervading their consciousness and presenting information at a rapid pace. It overstimulates the brain, which is incredibly unhealthy. Brain scientists argue that when information is presented more gradually, as through play or experimentation, we become organically interested in those ideas and more willing to explore a situation. This exploration feeds the imagination and helps children naturally become more inquisitive.

The incessant play and replay of images and stimuli on a screen leaves no room for children to be bored. This might sound like a good thing—but think again. The bulk of research evidence now confirms that boredom restores and revives the imagination, leading us to become more creative. Children can use their unoccupied time to create a dance routine or use notebook pages and crayons to make an airplane. Simply letting children play alone or look out the window while in a car is important for their brains—and therefore essential for their future lives as activists.

Not only does heavy television curtail curiosity, it negatively affects our children's executive functioning. Executive function is a set of mental skills, which includes having the ability to memorize, being flexible in our thinking, as well as demonstrating self-control. Children are not born with these skills—they are born with the *potential* to develop them. Some children may need more support than others to develop these skills. Executive function and self-regulation skills enable us to plan, focus our attention, remember instructions, and juggle multiple tasks successfully. The Center on the Developing Child at Harvard University describes the process in this way: "Just as an air traffic control system at a busy airport safely manages the arrivals and departures of many aircraft on multiple runways, the brain needs executive functioning skill sets to filter distractions, prioritize tasks, set and achieve goals, and control impulses." Many behaviors in which humans engage, such as breathing or swallowing, occur without conscious thought. But most others rely on executive function. Any process or goal pursuit that requires time management, decision-making, and storing information in one's memory uses executive function to some degree.

Being indoors in front of a screen is not good for children—for that matter, it is not good for any of us—and it can disrupt children's executive functioning. Though children can learn a lot indoors from books and playing with crayons, they can also learn a lot from being outdoors. Studies have shown that people who spend time outdoors, unplugged in nature, solve problems more creatively. For years scholars like experimental psychologist David Strayer of the University of Utah have been encouraging us to embrace nature. Being in the outdoors, he argues, quiets the prefrontal cortex and allows the brain to utilize some of its underutilized networks. The prefrontal cortex is like our imagination network: It's activated when we're not focusing on anything specific. You know it is on and working when you experience sudden flashes of insight. Being in nature, as opposed to being in a structured, indoor environment, allows such flashes to occur with greater frequency, thereby allowing us to be more creative and less stressed. The activity of the imagination network is absolutely vital to creativity. It draws on many regions across the brain, including the hippocampus. It enables us to consider other perspectives and scenarios, imagine the future, remember the past, understand ourselves and others, and create meaning from our experiences.

One way we create such meaning is through questioning. We have always gotten excited whenever Marley asks "Why?" after Scott or I assert something as fact. Questioning is a uniquely powerful tool because it spurs learning. By asking questions, we can improve our understanding. Encouraging questioning infuses learning with the true spirit of the scientific method—which is anchored in curiosity and critical thinking, two key foundational skills for a change-maker.

In his article "The Value of Asking Questions" molecular scientist Ronald Vale discusses the history of questions. He found: "In the Prashna-Upanishad, one of the earliest of the Upanishad texts that serve as a foundation of Hinduism, pupils pose six great questions to a wise teacher (*prashna* means question in Sanskrit). The Buddha also encouraged questioning by his disciples, and a fundamental role for questioning is still embraced in the practices of modern Buddhism." Scholars agree that questions have value because they are excellent vehicles with which to start a process of inquiry—a process that does not require a laboratory, special equipment, or money.

By encouraging questions, caregivers can aid children in their personal quest to resolve a point of curiosity or grapple with understanding an issue. One question often results in a further round of questions that dig deeper into a phenomenon. This engagement can lead children to want to know more, encouraging them to become thirsty for information. This thirst can then be used to promote independent learning. Furthermore, by supporting the art of questioning, parents alleviate themselves from being seen as the almighty vessel of knowledge who imparts information. We can also help children understand that sometimes questions have no immediate answer or an uncertain answer.

Parents should find this process exciting, because it means that arousing curiosity in children will better prepare them to learn lessons that they might otherwise consider difficult or even boring. Curiosity is connected to analytic abilities, problem-solving skills, and intelligence. In short, by encouraging curiosity in your child, you can make your kid smarter.

Curiosity is also a bonus when we are working to raise a change-maker, because the work of building curiosity begins with fostering *critical thinking*. Critical thinking is a reflective, analytical style of thinking that lies in understanding and applying logic, reasoning, and creating instead of learning by rote—and is the bedrock of problem-solving. And change-makers are problem solvers. Critical thinking is not an innate ability, however. We must teach children to actively consider and evaluate information, identify biases, examine the logic of arguments, and tolerate ambiguity.

So, what does that mean? It means delving deeper and asking questions like: Why is that so? Is this a good argument? What are other explanations? Further, having strong critical-thinking skills means being able to make decisions based on data, all while understanding its inherent uncertainties and variability.

Critical-thinking skills also stimulate your girl's imagination and teach her to identify patterns in the world, ultimately helping her to discover her own answers to some of society's most intractable questions and training her to recognize that frustration is useful and uncertainty acceptable. She begins to understand that learning can happen anywhere and everywhere, all the time, not just in a class-room.

The bottom line is that we *want* our girls to embrace uncertainty. Because for all the critical thinking, creativity, and facts we can teach our girls, we cannot predict the future—nor can we teach them to do so. We want them to learn that being an adult doesn't mean having all the answers. One of the best things we can do for our girls is to admit when we do not know something, then help them generate questions and seek answers. When we are seen as curious, they have permission to be curious too.

Further, we want our girls to know that there is more than one answer to most questions. Being comfortable with uncertainty helps create solutions. We want them to understand that when solving a problem we cannot guarantee the outcome; we can only consider the reasonableness of a solution.

One of our tasks in facilitating this type of curiosity is making it clear to your girl that life is organized by the social forces around her, such as her race and gender, where she lives, and where she goes to school. We can help her gain clarity on how these forces operate and how they might be working for or against her. We can sharpen her lens so that she can see the multiple ways that sexism, racism, and classism singularly and in combination shape and influence her life, and we can help her brainstorm what she can do about it.

Part of the work of raising a social activist is helping children become aware of the links between their individual choices and life conditions as well as the circumstances that shape their "sociological imagination." This term coined by C. Wright Mills exists to help us identify the interconnections between personal history and social forces—that is, to understand how those things around us influence our behaviors and values. Of course, one doesn't need a degree in sociology to understand that some problems are self-inflicted and that other problems are created by systems and structures and have become institutionalized. But for our children to understand the difference between individual problems and social issues, we must teach them to identify general patterns among large groups of people living in the same society who are experiencing the same societal pressures. Once children keenly understand how their actions and thoughts connect to society, they are well on their way to imaginatively solving some of our most intractable social problems.

At camp, we use examples from girls' lives to make these concepts real for them. Girls travel from across Essex County, New Jersey, to participate in our program. The county as a whole is very wealthy, boasting a median household income of $63,368, which is more than the median annual income of $61,937 across the entire United States. But that wealth is not evenly divided. The average income of a Newark resident is $16,828, while its neighbors in South Orange enjoy a household median income of $83,611. Girls may not know these numbers, but they observe the differences between these two communities, even though they may not understand why such differences exist. To help girls make sense of this economic disparity in neighborhoods, I ask them to notice what they see while driving with their parents. Are some streets cleaner than others? During the winter, which neighborhood streets are well plowed and which are not? Which communities have houses close together and which have more space between houses? En route to camp, where do you see more police? Often they point out things that I don't notice. They make note that McDonald's in some neighborhoods offers veggie burgers as an option while others don't. Schools in South Orange have large playgrounds and many in Newark do not.

Girls are also asked to look for and name patterns of things that occur within their schools and families. They sometimes point out patterns in the books they read or in who the teacher calls on. Once we have lists of these patterns, girls develop explanations about why these differences exist. This is where the hard work from hypothesis testing to refinement begins.

It's a lot, I know. But teaching our girls to understand how social forces shape how resources are allocated is critical. Understanding these forces and considering what action is needed are important matters in creating a change-maker. Don't worry, she doesn't need to get it all in one year, one sitting, or one moment. Understanding how things work and observing patterns of social behavior takes time; it's an ongoing process of learning, unlearning, questioning, and imagining. Our role as caregivers in this process is helping her to be curious about the world, encouraging her to ask *why*. Why are things the way they are? Why do I believe what I do? Why do I do the things that I do?

On top of teaching them these skills, we must fight the conventional notion that our children, particularly our girls, should just accept what is. If we do not think with conscious consideration, we can stifle girls' curiosity and risk-taking by shutting down their questions. We can limit the possibility that they become changemakers by pushing them toward drone-like acceptance of society's messaging. Rather, we should encourage them to investigate their own ideas and examine the world around them.

Too often, we punish girls' inquisitiveness and sense of exploration by calling them nosy. Indeed, parenting can be a power rush for some of us, so much so that our homes become oligarchies. Our religious beliefs, our sexual preferences, or our desires can operate less like guides and more like dictates. How we raise our children can oppress them or liberate them. So challenge yourself here to listen to your girl's questions without fear, and without your own prejudices. Remember, "Our imagination goes ahead of us, bringing our yesterday's imaginings into present realities" (Ogwo David Emenike).

ASSIGNMENTS

Read to fuel girls' imaginations.

What to read?
As soon as she can choose, let your girl make reading choices. Children learn best when they get to lead, and deciding what to read should be their choice. Having choice, they are more likely to be enthusiastic. Read the books she loves, not the ones you love. Yes, it is okay if she gravitates toward one genre of

books, and it is okay if she only likes one or two books and wants to read them over and over again. Do not push her to read at some imagined grade level. Introduce options, but follow her lead. She can read picture books, comic books, graphic novels, computer magazines. All reading is good.

When and for how long should you read?
Even on the day you are most tired, still read to her. The more you read, the more she reads, and a better reader she will become. Educators recommend reading to your girl at least fifteen to twenty minutes each day from birth. Read at any time in the day; if she likes you to read to her in the morning, then do so. Read when it is fun for both of you.

Where to read?
Choose reading locations that feel comfortable. Encourage her to read in the car, read with her in the living room, read together at the table, read menus at restaurants (always give her her own menu), read in your room or her room. Reading is a fun activity, not a chore, so you should do it everywhere. Just like you might take a few minutes out of your day to listen to your favorite song, take a few minutes each day to stop, drop, and read.

How to read?
When you are reading, treat it like a performance, paying attention to your tone of voice—vary it as much as possible. Be deliberate about your volume and intonations (e.g., don't be afraid to be dramatic; use your exclamation marks).

Build a home exploration curriculum.

Take an inventory of your skills and talents and share them with your children. Look for fun ways to incorporate learning into your daily life.

Grab some learning place mats, packs of playing cards, small plastic containers, mini shovels, plastic gloves, aprons, a large white mini easel, outdoor chalk, paint brushes, and markers from your local arts and craft store. I always recommend getting a music keyboard and a mini trampoline when she gets old enough. Put them all together so you always have a collection of fun things to play with. Also, keeping them together will make them easy to access when you want to do games and activities together. The activities should be so simple that you can incorporate them into your life without much fuss. When your child is young, you can do them at the kitchen table, on road trips, or on playdates.

Reading development
- Play the alphabet game: Name an animal (or other noun) that begins with the letter A, B, C . . .
- Teach spelling while on the swing or on the trampoline. Make it a game. The longer the word she can spell, the higher you will push her.

Math
- Teach her how to play blackjack really early. Learning how to get to twenty-one is a lot of fun. It also will help her learn which numbers have greater value. And it will help with algebra in the future. The face cards take on a value that is assigned to them. Though it may be abstract to them now, it will become clear by the time they have to learn these concepts.
- Hopscotch is a great way to learn math. Using the sidewalk, she can learn to count or she can hop onto prime numbers.

Art
Coloring is among one of the most peaceful activities. You can color while waiting at the doctor's office, at the airport, or in the car. Always have a box of crayons on you. At all ages it is the perfect way to engage the imagination, talk colors, and calm the spirit.

Music
A mini-keyboard provides hours of fun. She can make her own music, or she can play recorded music. Musical instrument sets

have all the supplies one needs for creating all kinds of music. Your girl can be her own band, or when family and friends are around, each person can become a member of the band.

Explore nature together.

Engaging with nature invites questioning because we know so little about how nature works. Encourage her to find an insect, plant, or bird. Take a picture while you are in nature and then ask her to research it and share her findings with you. Question her about her findings, and see if you can both expand the inquiry even further.

Give your child a chance to reflect.

When in conversation with her, try counting (silently) to sixty while your girl is thinking before intervening. Let her think and speak without feeling rushed. This will give her a chance to reflect on and perhaps refine her response, rather than responding with her first gut reaction.

Ask open-ended questions.

Rather than automatically giving answers to the questions your child raises, help her think critically by asking questions in return:

- What ideas do you have?
- What do you think is happening here?

Respect her responses whether you view them as correct or not. You could say: "That is interesting. Tell me why you think that." Use phrases like "I would love to hear your thinking about this," "How would you solve this problem?," or "Say more so I can better understand."

Invite friends and family to participate in a weekly questions contest.

Reward the person who asks the most intriguing question. This will show your girl that questions are as important as answers. Albert Einstein was known to be a genius, but as he famously explained: "I have no special talents. I am only passionately curious."

Get informed about misinformation.

As I outlined in Chapter 8, misinformation, often appearing in the form of unsubstantiated opinions, is now rampant in our society. In addition to reviewing Luvvie Ajayi's "5 Things to Do to Avoid Passing on Fake News on Social Media," I suggest you review Georgetown University Library's article on "Evaluating Internet Resources." It provides a comprehensive list of questions that you should ask when getting information from the Web. Children must know that the responsibility is on the user to evaluate resources effectively; therefore, they must be able to discern fact from fiction.

Adopt a learning mindset.

Seize opportunities to learn. Model for your girl by saying, "Let's figure it out." This openness to learning, with all the discomfort and excitement it can entail, can be infectious. The process starts with asking *why.* There may not be a reason why everything is the way it is, but asking questions will almost always lead to interesting revelations about life.

Coach your girl in developing good questions that can build knowledge of herself and the world. You should adopt the motto: "There is no stupid question. Stupid people don't ask questions." — Unknown

12

Create a Space to Hear Her Voice

~~~~~~

You will not be able to hear her questions if you do not create a space to hear her voice. If she is rendered mute, she will not want to explore and she will not share her ideas. We must fight against this silencing of girls. I understand this far too well.

I was eight years old, living with my grandmother and many members of our extended family under one roof, including my Aunt Joyce and her daughter Carol. Carol and I were very close growing up. Born four months apart, we spent most of our days together, and I both admired and resented her. She was faster, stronger, and prettier than I was. Her skin was reddish like the clay dirt of our hillside. My resentment came from the fact that Carol got to live with her mom, sister, and brother and had an ongoing relationship with her dad—while I had never met my father and barely remembered my mother, who was working overseas and left when I was only two years old. I envied Carol's secure place within our family, especially since in my view my Aunt Joyce, her mother, took every opportunity to favor her, always serving her first dinner and washing and ironing her clothes before mine.

In the absence of both my parents, I fantasized about being someone's favorite. But with no one to put me first, I had to become my own best friend. I learned to live almost entirely within my imagination. One of my preferred pursuits was to collect and play with Seville oranges that had fallen from their branches and lay neglected on the ground. I'd throw them high in the air and try to catch them, or I'd kick them across the yard, pretending to be star soccer player Pelé. I loved the feel of their round, dimpled skins, their bright color in the sun.

One day, Carol snatched one of the oranges I had been playing with. I asked her to return it, but she refused. I was incensed; I could feel anger roaring inside my head. I was clearly more irate than I needed to be, but in the moment my frustration seemed justifiable, principled. Carol could have picked up any number of Seville oranges of her own—there were plenty lying around—but instead, she felt entitled to take mine. The next thing I knew, I had pushed my cousin into the bushes and stomped away. Carol ran to my grandmother's house and tattled on me. That afternoon, Aunt Joyce spanked me roundly and then banished me to time-out under the dining table. This was a standard punishment. It was also commonplace that no one asked the reason for my actions. It did not occur to her to ask *why* I had behaved so badly. And it did not occur to me to try to explain. I huddled under the table for the allotted time, watching mealworms and cockroaches crawl through a pile of spilled flour on the floor as I imagined a life where adults listened to my side of the story.

I had borne the brunt of what felt like unjustified and unequal treatment for as long as I could remember, and anger had built up inside me. And yet I felt muted. Experience had shown me that my family, like so many, was deaf to my voice and blind to my unique reality, so what was the point of speaking up? Unfortunately, my habit of silence had only hardened their lack of interest in anything I had to say. Trapped in what seemed like a cycle, I felt like I had no voice. The habit of keeping most of my feelings or ideas to myself stayed with me until I got to college. My aunt and grandmother and later my mother and brothers had no real sense of what I thought. I rarely shared any of my feelings, thoughts, or passions with them. From the outside I appeared obedient, but inside I had so much to express. I simply did not.

In college I had to perpetually share my ideas. My new American environment, including an onslaught of daytime TV show hosts like Oprah Winfrey, Phil Donahue, and Sally Jessy Raphael, meant that everyone was emoting, and I was going to have to emote too. Everywhere I went I was asked about my feelings. It felt exhausting at first, but the more I did it the more I came to see its value. Sharing my feelings and opinions was the pathway to finding my voice.

Since then, I have come to learn and understand that it is so *important* to help our girls find their voices. This chapter will offer strategies for doing just that. Because whether pursuing constructive resolutions to conflict or charging forth to change the world, a girl must be confident that her voice matters, and she must allow space for other people's voices. Furthermore, she needs to be able to convey her emotions and discuss her feelings about things happening to and around her. This ability will help her when it is time to speak up about issues of injustice, and it will also help her when it is time to speak her truth to those in authority—even if that authority is you.

Let me tell you about one of our original GrassROOTS Super-Girls, a quiet girl named Tori, who used to believe that her voice didn't matter. At school, her teachers never called on her, even though she usually had the highest test scores in her class. As far back as she could remember, she was always one of only two Black girls in her grade—and in her school—and hers was the only Black family on her suburban street. At home, she refused to hug her relatives or even say hello. Her mother, Sonia, a history teacher, lamented her daughter's sullen mood, which she interpreted as rudeness and extreme shyness.

In her first and second years at SuperCamp, Tori was reticent and at times seemed disengaged, but her mom insisted she was having a good time and kept sending her to camp. We included Tori in all activities and projects, but she often balked at participating and shied away from all public presentations. Tori didn't attend camp in year three because her grandmother had been diagnosed with breast cancer, and the family opted to spend the summer near her in South

Carolina. She joined us again for year four, and that's when the seeds we had patiently planted started to bear fruit.

Tori's fourth year was a critically important year because we shifted our curriculum to focus keenly on girls' leadership development, specifically teaching them to identify issues of systemic inequity. In between drum lessons and art and poetry classes, our girls participated in workshops, attended lectures, watched videos, and learned more about the history of how racism and sexism operate. We also held workshops on how to address bullying and how to respond to microaggressions, such as when someone touches your hair without your permission; we make sure that we have many robust youth-generated dialogues about beauty and body. These workshops, led largely by master's- and doctoral-level scholars, were the ones that piqued ten-year-old Tori's interest.

While she was away from camp that one summer, she had missed the camaraderie of the girls she had known for two years. Also, she had spent the previous school years in a space where she felt alone. Now she was excited to return. Camp was a time to connect with girls who were like her. Tori described the key moments that helped her come out of her shell: being back in a safe space, repeating her affirmation, attending a workshop on hieroglyphics, and an affirming community circle discussion. Tori described a workshop on hieroglyphs by Dr. Sandra Lewis, then camp co-director and Professor of Psychology and Director of the African American Studies program at Montclair State University, and how much it impacted her. Hieroglyphics, the formal writing system used by ancient Egyptians to record their stories and history, was also used as writing to record everyday things. Dr. Lewis detailed for the girls how this early civilization's communication system used pictures. The writing looked like beautiful art. A single picture symbol could stand for a whole word, called an ideogram, or a sound, called a phonogram. For example, a picture of an eye could mean the word *eye* or the letter *I*. Since writing in hieroglyphics was so complicated, it took years of education and practice to be able to do it. Children as young as six or seven would train for years to become scribes.

Tori was excited to learn about this subject because she realized she could take this knowledge back to school and none of her peers would likely know about this. She could use this information to impress her teachers and other students. Camp community conversations aided her to find her voice. During these morning exchanges, girls often talked about their home and school experiences. We discussed issues and worked through matters. Hearing other girls' experiences of being overlooked by their teachers or feeling uncomfortable showed her she was neither crazy nor alone. Equally important to her was a conversation she and I had about how she came to find her voice. She said, "You gave the thing that I was experiencing a name. I didn't have the words before. I thought I was just shy, but I wasn't shy. I didn't want to talk because no one was listening to me. I didn't feel safe." As she began to feel safer, loved, and valued, she was able to talk and share more.

It was a dramatic shift. Tori became visibly more confident. Suddenly, she wanted to participate in every activity—from her group's talent show and nature walks to mentoring meetings with women trailblazers, many of whom she'd avoided talking with before. She began to open up, becoming more articulate and expressive about her ideas. No longer shy and sullen, she asked her mother and father not to send her back to her predominantly white public school. Her mother was surprised, but after Tori described years of feeling isolated and ignored at school—teachers never choosing her for awards, students never inviting her to birthday parties, and teams always choosing her last for games—her mother understood. "I finally got that what I've been experiencing is racism," Tori told her mother. Hearing stories of the microaggressions that her daughter had experienced was a blow to her parents. "Why didn't she tell us?" her mother asked me. "Why didn't she complain to someone at the school? Why did she keep these issues to herself?" Her parents wanted answers to all these questions. But the question at the root of all those other questions was: What else had they missed in Tori's life? After some courageous conversations, her parents agreed to move her to a smaller, more diverse school. Her parents hustled to find a place for her and enrolled her in a new school for the fall. A part of understanding Tori's story lies in understanding her mother's perspective. Sonia, her mother, is a teacher and like so many of us believed that teachers are right and children are often wrong. She had not considered that the school environment and the actions of the teachers could be the sources of Tori's "shyness" or discomfort. By sitting in the community circle and hearing other children discuss their injuries and mistreatments at school and by taking the time to talk and listen to Tori, she finally heard Tori's complaint, enough to take it seriously and to take action.

At the end of the summer, Tori's peers voted her SuperCamp Champion, a special recognition given by the campers to a peer who made a significant impact on others and showed growth over the course of the camp. I was so proud of her. The progress she had made just drove home to me that as we create ample opportunities for girls to express their truths, we will see them and their ideas grow. And Tori really did grow. The following year she decided that she wanted to spend her time helping underprivileged children in Newark. With support from her family and friends, Tori organized a basketball game where the entrance fee was a winter coat for a youth in need. I wish you could have seen this once-shy girl standing alone, confident, in the middle of the basketball court and announcing to a group of over one hundred participants why this work mattered to her.

At her new school, Tori has become more socially integrated and has more friends. Once a wallflower, today Tori's warmth toward others is freely expressed in hugs, and she is a sought-after leader in SuperCamp. All those years when she wasn't talking, she was observing her own unequal treatment. She just didn't have the words to explain what was going on and how it made her feel. Like eight-year-old me, she felt that silence was the only way to protest the injustice. Tori's story begs the question: How do we encourage our girls to share with us what is *really* happening in their lives?

As you know, I think it is so important to listen to our children's desires. The listening activities discussed in Part 2 should be repeated, this time with the aim of finding out more about your girl's life. We also need to help our girls find their unique voices and points of view so that they can be comfortable talking about difficult issues. Giving and creating space for children's voices is not just about listening. It is about emboldening them, allowing them to speak for themselves whenever possible. It demands that we let them be the expert on their own emotions and of the meanings they give to things.

Furthermore, we must help them find the words to understand how social issues are affecting their daily lives and arm them with the vocabulary to name and discuss social inequities.

To address these issues, we must consider the ways we create space for our girls' voices. I'm not talking about the sound that comes out of their mouths—I'm talking about *voice,* an expression of your girl's identity—herself and her emotions. A key goal of helping children have a voice is to deepen our awareness of how children's emotions help and hinder their ability to express themselves. If a girl does not believe that her opinion matters and it makes no difference what she thinks because all things are predetermined, then she is not likely to share her ideas. In youth development studies, the concept of voice centers on how children tell their own stories, and how they make sense of what happens to them. Our task as caregivers is to help children have ownership of themselves and their actions and to encourage them to feel like they are the main characters of their lives. It's not necessarily an easy task.

Scholars at the University of Melbourne argue that "our cognitive cocoons and our own adult emotional responses . . . can lead not only to us projecting on to the child what their meaning of an experience might be, but also to censoring the child's meaning." Oftentimes, we as adults will tell our girls what they should feel rather than help them make sense of what they feel. The solution: Stop that and listen. Youth development scholars urge us to move away from deciding for our children the meaning of their experiences and instead listen to children as current, not just future, citizens and let their voices be heard and acted upon now.

However, listening is easier than acting on the information they provide us, because even when we make room for our children's opinion, our instinct is often just to note what they have said and move on. Instead, I am suggesting that we choose to act on our newfound understanding. I find that one of the hardest things about being a parent is putting aside my own opinions and making room for my child's—and then incorporating this new understanding in my daily engagement with her.

As caregivers, we sometimes feel like our opinions should often, if not always, reign supreme—after all, we are older, we have more experience, and we have a longer relationship with the world around us. But regardless of how you feel about an issue, creating a confident kid means consistently listening to and considering your child's opinions—on *everything*. That means you must be more than tolerant; you must embrace the fact that, because of their youth and relative inexperience, they may be deeply underinformed and impulsive. But that doesn't necessarily mean they are *wrong*. And you must leave open the possibility that there is something to learn from listening to and understanding your child's point of view; consider what their fresh—albeit naïve—take has to offer.

Yes, they may be self-centered and focused primarily on getting their way. (Remember, as adults we often want to have our way too.) However, telling your child, "I know better" is hardly ever the solution. Because, as Bob Marley put it, "he who feels it knows it." Children know best what they feel, so we must empower them to express that which is true for them. Research shows that if we want to have agentic children, we must allow them to make choices and share their feelings about what happens around them. We must do as educational scholars Kevin Burke and Stuart Greene suggest, "Provide opportunities for young people to speak freely, safe spaces for them to speak their mind and reveal their truths and confront their truths no matter how convenient or inconvenient they might be, for others or for themselves."

In my own parenting thus far, I have struggled with not listening closely enough. Yet, I keep trying, and failing, and trying again; you must too. I have tried hard to make room for my daughter's opinions. I didn't want to be one of those parents who lets their child dictate everything, but I was also overly concerned about the potential that I could be like my aunt and grandma who failed to encourage *my* voice. Over time, I compromised: I offered my guidance while also allowing my daughter to discover and refine her own perspective and ideas. At the heart of my strategy is making room for her opinions in an age-appropriate way—teaching her very early to have a point of view and then respecting her perspective and decisions. This process started early. Her dad and I worked from day one to create a household that embraces democratic concepts and skills that are essential for respectful, egalitarian social relationships.

To be clear, we do not share authority with our girl, but instead we do what political scientist John Gastil suggests: We provide a learning environment in which she can understand the value of the democratic process, develop healthy relationships with us and her friends, and learn how to speak and listen in a deliberative manner. Here's how:

When Marley was under five years old, I distilled every decision down to two or three choices. I might ask if she preferred pizza or soup for lunch. Or I would say, "Do you want to wear pants, a dress, or a skirt today?" Then, based on her response, I would select three outfits and she would choose one. For activities, I might ask, "Do you want to go to the mall with me or do you want to stay at home with Dad?" In each case she had an opportunity to develop a point of view and select a preference but with limitations. Having choices made her understand that her opinion was valuable and that she was the author of her own story; also, she got to make those choices without the pressure of creating the entire framework for her life. We very consciously taught her to use her voice so that she would feel like the main character in her life.

If letting your girl pick out her own clothes seems like a hassle, or like it's not going to make a huge difference to her, please reconsider. Too often, parents select their child's clothing without considering the child's ideas about how she wants to appear. Or, they inform their children that they are going somewhere without leaving room for any input, with the result that kids often feel dragged along. Then, when children are asked their opinion about something, they have no experience of discerning what they think or feel. The same parents who offered them no room for developing a clear point of view will sometimes punish or demean their children for not speaking up. These parents have made their children bystanders in their own lives, and when they are suddenly asked to be upstanders, they do not know where to begin. They've never been coached to develop the skill of interrogating themselves and deciding what matters to them.

Social scientists Shlomit Oryan and John Gastil advise that we, as guardians and parents, develop democratic habits and capacities in our children. They suggest that we use every opportunity to enable our children to make decisions for themselves by involving them in family decision-making and listening to their opinions while agreeing to consider their ideas. Fundamentally, they suggest that parents clarify the special responsibilities that will come with gradual emancipation from their parents' concentrated authority and ready their children for autonomous democratic citizenship. These start with embracing children's questions.

I remember when my mother taught me the value of being heard. Now, to be fair, my mother didn't necessarily enjoy hearing my opinions—it wasn't so much about that—but over the years she has created a fair amount of space for me to share my ideas.

When my brothers and I left Jamaica to live with my mother in Boston, she worked around the clock in order to provide for us. When she was home on Sundays, she mostly cooked. She had a weekly routine. She would toil in the kitchen for hours making a full week's worth of meals—one big pot of rice and peas, another pot of white rice, sautéed liver with onions, steamed cabbage, a pan of shake-and-bake chicken, a pot of stew chicken, and spaghetti and meatballs, plus some other quintessentially American food. After creating several days' worth of dinners, she would make a plate for every member of the family. She would lay the plates on the counter to cool before wrapping them in aluminum foil. Then, with markers, she would write each of our names on top.

Sitting at the table watching her, I noticed that she always made my stepfather Cecil's plate first. *Why should he always be first?* I wondered. There was no conceivable reason.

Finally, I asked her: "Why do you share out Cecil's food before ours?"

"Do I?" she responded. There was surprise in her voice.

"Yes, you always do!" I said, irritated that she had never noticed. She paused and looked at me thoughtfully. "I don't know," she admitted, confirming that it wasn't a conscious act. I told her that I thought it was unfair because we were her children and we came from her. So why should Cecil, who at that time was not even her husband, always get better treatment?

At that point, my mother stopped what she was doing and sat down with me. She confessed that when she was a child in Jamaica, it had bothered her that Gifford, my grandmother's husband, always got his food before the children. And Gifford got larger portions than anyone else, as well as better food. She marveled that she had somehow failed to see that she was doing the same thing her mother had done.

And just like that, on a Sunday afternoon in 1984 when I was twelve years old, my mother stopped feeding her children last. But what was more critical to my dawning sense of self was that she had taken the time to hear me out and to explore with me how it must have felt to witness this way of life in Jamaica, and how it must feel to watch it now. She listened to my feelings while also sharing her own. It was a powerful affirmation for me: My mother had demonstrated that my voice, specifically my point of view, mattered, and in so doing made it clear that *I* mattered to her.

This moment was redemptive for me and my mother. Regardless of our frequent disagreements, in this moment she was my salvation. By listening to and attending to my concern about this matter, my mother bolstered my sense of self, and that experience stayed with me today and remains valuable in the way I parent today. She allowed me to express how I was feeling freely, even in the midst of this uncomfortable conversation.

Encouraging children to express themselves in their own words, affording them the opportunity to discuss their anxieties, fears, demands, and dreams with adults, enhances intergenerational communication, laying the foundation for future courageous conversations. These skills are vital for change-makers, particularly because children are morally and intellectually less competent to judge and deliberate on their own interests. They need to work with and learn from guardians and parents for whom they have mutual respect. They need to hear their loved one's perspectives so that they can understand their humanity, thoughts, and ideas. These are the central principles of developing respect for others. That respect begins with creating a space where we as caregivers listen and learn from their voices and share our feelings. It is within these exchanges that girls get to see models of leadership that they can use to create safe spaces and advocate for others.

ASSIGNMENTS

Ask open-ended questions to help you better understand what she is thinking and feeling.

Children often pose questions that challenge us. Sometimes they force us to confront a truth that we were not ready to share. But if we want curious, engaged children, we must encourage them to speak confidently. Their questions and insights give us a chance to clear up any confusion and make our values and ideas understood. The questions children ask offer a window into their thinking.

What not to do:
"How was school?"
    "Was today good?"
    "Did you learn anything at school today?"
    These are close-ended questions that require only a yes or no response.

What to do instead:

"Tell me about your day."

Always ask open-ended questions that invite conversation. Then follow up:

"What was the best part of your day?"

"What would you like to teach me today?" This question invites your girl to be the leader.

"What would you change if you could?"

Then probe for why:

"What would you like to happen tomorrow?"

"What can you do differently to make that happen?"

"What can I do to support you in that? What would you like me to do to help you get ready for school tomorrow?"

Carve out time for intentional conversations.

Mute the television or silence your phone when your girl is talking to you. We are often very busy as we go about our days, multitasking at work, at home, or parenting. Pausing can feel like a luxury, but it is important that we stop and listen. Interrupting the daily routine is an opportunity to affirm your girl and hear her ideas. When she feels she is heard, she will share more with you.

Offer her choices so she can develop a point of view.

From early in life, children need to be able to tune in to their likes and dislikes. Talk to them about choices and making informed decisions. Present them with options so you can assess the calculus they are using to make decisions. Their input does not guarantee they will get their way, but at least their preferences will be known and can be weighed in the decision-making process. Here are some examples:

- Food choices: Which vegetables would you like to have with dinner? Would you like pasta or chicken for dinner?
- Family obligations: We have to go to Grandma's this weekend; would you rather go on Friday or Saturday?
- Conflicting options: It is Friday night after a long week of school. Your child has a project due Monday, but a party invite for Saturday at one o'clock. Ask: Would you like to do your homework on Friday after dinner, wake up at ten o'clock on Saturday to work on the project, or leave the party early to come home and complete your homework? (You can also let your child know the pros and cons of each decision.)

> - **Choice 1: Homework tonight after the party.** You are most likely going to be tired when you get back and may not give your homework your best thinking. This could negatively impact your grade and/or insult your teacher.
> - **Choice 2: Go to party and wake up early on Saturday.** You typically sleep until the afternoon on Saturday. If you go to the party, you will have to set your alarm and wake up several hours earlier. Also, you may rush homework so that you have enough time to get dressed for the party.
> - **Choice 3: Go to party and leave early.** You might be having a good time at the party and not want to leave.

Talk with her about which choices allow her the best chance of meeting her personal and social obligations. Do not assume she knows because the choice is clear to you. Laying out for her the pros and cons will help her evaluate between competing options. She needs to understand that no one choice will be perfect. Choices are about decision-making and judgment.

13

Cultivate Her Passions

Listening to others is invaluable, but it is equally important to listen to your inner voice. It will lead you to what matters to you the most. I know so far I have described myself as a person of conviction and action, but prior to my daughter's birth, I might not have labeled myself as having specific passions—and certainly not any useful enough to powerfully impact the world. In truth, for as long as I can remember, I only wanted to be good at the high jump and at sprinting. I did love watching television as a teenager, but I was not interested in acting, directing, or producing. I liked dancing, but I sucked at it, and I certainly was not interested in spending hours trying to improve. Mastery was not prized in my household. We were expected to do our best in school and that was enough. My mother was not concerned about grades or any specific occupation. Her desire for us was simple: Grow up so that you can take care of yourself.

High school changed things for me. When my mom finally allowed me to go to the public library—something she objected to for years—I discovered I loved investigating what others had written; I spent hours searching through microfiche and looking up newspaper articles. I also enjoyed combing through books and was captivated by reading stories, political essays, and op-eds. I was curious about the various positions people took on the same types of questions or issues. During that time, I also realized that compiling evidence to support an argument was exciting to me. It wasn't long before this interest led me to join the debate and mock trial teams. By senior year I had many new passions, and I wanted to be good at the things that I loved. For the first time I had a desire to gain mastery.

Despite these experiences, however, I would not have specifically said I had any noteworthy passions. Furthermore, for most of my adult life, I have been occupationally agnostic, never desiring or wanting to have a specific job title. After graduating from college, I taught high school in Newport, Rhode Island, not because I had a deep abiding passion for teaching—well, at least that's what I thought—but because I needed a job and was determined not to return to my mother's house. In Rhode Island, though, I lived on Purgatory Road, and for more reasons than one, I felt like I was in a state of constant incompleteness. So, I left my nicely paid teaching job in the comfort of Newport for graduate school, pursuing a graduate degree without knowing what one *does* with a graduate degree in sociology. At that point, it was clear that I had drive, but I didn't know where I was *going*.

Luckily, by the time my daughter came along, I had a clearer sense of myself and my passions. Marley was born to a mom who was (and is) a researcher. I was now making a living out of my love for reading articles, summarizing articles and reports, and investigating ideas. I felt in my bones that it was important for her to see my passion and purpose in action, to see how following them fulfilled me. That's why I would take Marley along with me when I gave talks to community groups, government officials, and academics. She became a member of the GrassROOTS Community Foundation where for the past ten summers her mother has taught girls how to recite and perform poetry. In addition, she has run alongside her mother in multiple 5K races. My daughter knows me as the person who wakes up at 4:15 A.M. to go to the gym, where I am constantly trying to achieve a good running pace. She was there when I became a certified spin instructor. She sees me practice my talk and listens to me discuss my trials and errors in training. Simply, she knows she has a mom who has lots of passions. And, more important, she understands passion and purpose to be *inextricably linked.*

I strongly believe Marley has been inspired to cultivate her passions not just by watching me live a life guided by my own passions, but also by being exposed to a variety of activities and interests through the years.

In this book, I have asked you to be intentional about all areas of your parenting. Often I have told you that you need to enact rules and boundaries in order to do so. Here, however, I ask that you not limit the things your girl encounters or bridle her passions. Additionally, ignore popular ideas that suggest your child needs to have one unique passion, and block out comments from those who push you to monetize your child's passions. You are not cultivating your child's passions for any specific occupational, academic, or athletic goal. You are trying to raise a joyful child who can positively impact the world, regardless of what she does for a job, what specific subjects she excels in at school, or whether or not she makes it to the state championship or the Olympics. If we work to unearth our girls' passions so they can come into and appreciate their fullness and power, then they can feel efficacious enough to use that power to advance justice. It's good for the world and it's good for her too.

The pathway to this goal begins with tuning in to our girl's specific interests and becoming familiar with research evidence on using passion to guide our course of action.

First, a caveat: Academic scholars have a lot to say about passion, but few offer directed guidance to caregivers about how to support or bolster their children's passions. Psychologist Robert Vallerand from the University of Quebec at Montreal defines it as a strong inclination toward a self-defining activity that one likes, loves, or highly values, and in which one invests a significant amount of time and energy. Vallerand and colleagues propose that passion has two forms. The first kind of passion, "harmonious passion," comes from autonomous internalization of the activity, which means people will pursue these things on their own. They freely engage in an action because it aligns with their values and interests. In essence, this type of passion complements other aspects of themselves and leads them to experience high levels of concentration, positive affect, and enhanced energy. The second kind of passion, "obsessive passion," comes from a controlled internalization of an activity into one's identity, which leads people to experience an uncontrollable urge to engage in the activity and to feel controlled largely by external pressures. In case you can't tell, harmonious passion, which is driven by forces within, is the one we want to cultivate in our girls.

Harmonious passions will benefit your girl's overall well-being and facilitate her desire to create a more just world—regardless of external pressures. If that isn't motivation enough to make such passions a priority, all the available evidence suggests that harmonious passions predict dedication and internal peacefulness, namely joy. For parents, this is a real gift. With so much to do, imagine how wonderful it is when we don't have to prompt our children to do yet another thing. Their autonomy and dedication mean freedom for us.

Does this mean that once these passions have been cultivated our work is done as parents or that we should abdicate our role in supporting and cultivating our children's passions? No, that's not what I'm saying. But it *does* mean we have less work to do. Allow your girl to decide when and how she wants to engage with her passions. All you have to do is get her there. She'll do the rest.

But what can caregivers do about helping girls find and master their passions, if much of this motivation is self-generated?

Academic research provides some breadcrumbs in getting to the answer, but it does not provide specific instructions. However, scholars are clear that the answer lies in exposure and exploration. Expose your child to everything, and offer her a variety of interesting options. Early introductions to a variety of things will help even very young children have interests. As caregivers, we shape those interests by involving girls in fun, interesting, hands-on learning experiences that they can explore, expressing their own theories and understandings through a variety of representative mediums. For example, when your girl was young you watched her learn to roll or crawl, walk, and jump. She was determined to master the new skill, so she practiced and practiced. The happiness she felt from accomplishing this task may have exceeded your own. That type of motivation continues as she grows, and so might her interests. She may at times appear to be interested in everything and anything.

So despite your desire to reduce her interests and push her to focus, do *not* do that. It is okay for your girl to have a lot of interests. There are children who absolutely love everything they do and try. Maybe they have athletic talent, are quick-witted and able to pick up new things easily, and enjoy being active. Or maybe your girl is like Ayanna, a SuperGirl who loves science, singing, art, and ponies.

When they end up in a dilemma about which interests to choose as an extracurricular activity, they and you might both be frustrated. Consider helping them organize their options, rather than pushing them to curtail their interests. Children do not have to have a niche. They need not be experts. Reject the idea that passions are "fixed." Children tend to give up on new interests, particularly through adolescence. Encourage and embrace the variety of their choices.

A caveat: Being good at something does *not* mean your girl is passionate about it. Though it may frustrate you, it is critical that she leads in choosing which interests to pursue, not you. Just because you think she has a gift for something, does not mean that is the activity she should choose. That way lies danger.

I am not sure that if I were the one who chose Marley's primary activity I would have zeroed in on books. She's good at so many things; I enjoy watching her dance, and I love her poetry. But she chose books and reading. Marley *loved* books, reading, and bookstores as a child. I am not surprised, given how much time we spent in these settings. But the exposure did not determine her love. She was exposed to reading, and she gravitated toward it. What began as an activity led by me became a passion led by her. It was *her* passion and love of books that led her to follow her passion and become a social activist about reading.

Being a part of her process, I have learned that, as caregivers, we should understand that once a person becomes passionate about something, it can become a central feature of their identity and may even define them. For example, it can mean the difference between a person who runs and a person who is a runner. Regardless of what else the person does, running is a central part of their identity. Therefore, we must provide the space for our girls to come to and understand their own harmonious passions. Arriving at that path demands that we create a context whereby they can engage in this discovery with full autonomy to make choices.

The science instructs us that children's passions can be developed by supporting their autonomy, that is, the sense of performing an activity for themselves, without external pressures. Because they are in charge, they can maintain this harmonious passion even when facing difficult situations that impact their passion. When your girl gets to choose, she is better able to engage in an activity for long periods of time, thus contributing to improved ability.

Passion provides people with the energy and goals to engage in deliberate practice. Though harmonious passion may not singularly focus on goals, passion does facilitate goal achievement (something most every parent wants). That's because being passionate leads a person to engage fully in activities. Such deliberate practice leads to high performance attainment. Basically, if you focus not on the resulting outcome of an activity, but rather entirely on mastering the activity, you will usually not only achieve your goal, but excel at it.

Again, when people are driven by their passions they can engage in activities for extended periods of time; as an added bonus, this focused attention fosters mindfulness, which is said to positively affect mental and physical health. Mindfulness is associated with positive emotions and awareness of one's emotions.

I encourage you to create a mindfulness context in your homes. The central components of mindfulness—the ability to be present-centered (paying attention to and noticing what is happening *now*) and to be nonjudgmental (observing things as they are with a fully accepting attitude)—are hugely beneficial. Moreover, educational research scholars have observed that students who perceive their teachers to be encouraging, supportive, and caring are more passionate. Likewise, students are more likely to develop passion for activities that are congruous with their own interests when they have challenges and more opportunities for choice. Caregivers can replicate this behavior of teachers by giving their girls more and more space for discovery of their own interests and for opportunities to be challenged.

A core area of challenge for caregivers comes when your girl's passions meet her frustrations. As protectors of our children, we might intervene when we watch our girl get frustrated that she cannot master a thing or when she yells and screams during something she typically enjoys. I urge you—do not interrupt. Let her be frustrated (within reason).

In fact, many people have discovered their passion after encountering what they initially found as frustrating. Temporary feelings are precisely that—temporary. We must not ignore frustrations and uncomfortable emotions. Instead, caregivers can lean in on their children's frustrations because they are fuel for passions. They provide ignition, propelling your girl to be a social activist. If you and your girl can use your passions to address her frustrations and dissatisfaction about society, then you are well on your way to making the world a better place.

ASSIGNMENT

Help her identify her harmonious passions.

Notice your child's interests by paying attention to what makes her smile and laugh. Ask her what she likes. What does she like to do with her peers? Are there activities she could try with a friend?

- Ask trusted friends or family members what they observe about your girl—do they see that your girl has a special talent, or that something really seems to ignite her inner spark? Share their findings with her to see if she agrees.

- Show her you notice her passions and provide opportunities for her to pursue her interests. For example, if you notice that she likes animals, share with her television shows about animals, take her to a petting zoo, ask her if she would like to volunteer for a day at an animal shelter.
- Share your passion. Tell your girl about the things that you were passionate about when you were her age. What did you find enjoyable? Talk to her about the multiple hours of practice, study, or viewing that you did to engage your passions. Allow her to have a blueprint for how to think about her passions. (Note: This is where you must be prepared to talk about why you are no longer passionate about some things. This is also where you may have to reconcile with yourself and her the ways in which performance goals and jobs shaped your decision to not pursue some passions.)

Be the sunlight for helping her passions grow.

By providing the context for her to find her purpose, you may be helping her see that her passion and purpose can go hand in hand. This may be hard. Purpose comes from answering the question: What is greater than you that has captured your interest and your commitment?

14

Why We Lift as We Climb

Creating a better world requires that we lift as we climb, a lesson I learned early in my life. Every evening during my childhood, my grandmother and aunts would make huge pots of food for dinner, much more than was required to feed all thirteen of us. Each child would be given a heaping plate to take to our neighbors; the younger kids were sent out in pairs. My cousin Carol and I, at five and six years old, went together. We were told that the people to whom we brought the food were our family, and since they didn't have sufficient resources, it was our responsibility to share with them.

We children often complained. Yes, we were lazy in the way all kids are, and the food smelled delicious. And some neighbors were as far as two miles away! We wanted to be able to just sit down to eat, but that was not an option. My grandmother insisted that we deliver the dinners before we could have ours; you serve others before serving yourself. This routine of bringing dinner to folks in the community had been my grandmother's practice long before I was born, and the ritual of sharing our blessings with those in need continued until my grandmother passed away.

My grandmother's death was the most painful experience of my adult life. She had been my anchor, the woman who had known and loved me my whole life in ways that no one else would or could. Her slow demise was torturous for her and for the whole family. She fell ill and then into a coma, and when she emerged from it she was blind, fragile, and forgetful. I visited her in 1994, and she could barely remember me. Though her physical death came in 1999, I had started mourning her years earlier.

My grandmother's given name was Margaret Taylor-Gifford. Her mother had been an enslaved African who shared traditional West African tales of the spider Anansi and taught her daughter how to use herbs and the spirits to heal. My grandmother believed that the presence of God was made visible in our actions, and she taught us to honor God through service to family and community. Really, she protected me and showed me so much. Her actions and inactions, her views on women, and her relationships with her husband and children continue to offer me lessons in navigating the world. But like all of us, she was flawed, and even though I loved her deeply, I was and remain deeply critical of some of her parenting decisions—for example, not believing my mother, who was being sexually harassed at the age of twelve by the men in their village, and letting her leave home at *such* a young age.

Yet, despite my grandmother's flaws, she was perfectly, irrefutably beautiful in one way: She was steadfast in her generosity and conviction about giving and sharing blessings. She taught me that hoarding your resources when others are in need is a sin. She believed in uplifting those who were disenfranchised and that it was our responsibility to help others, despite our personal feelings about them. Liking the person you were helping was not a requirement; my grandmother maintained that all people deserve respect.

When she died, I was living in Harlem with Scott and had already earned my master's degree, which made me a symbol of success in the family. So, I was asked to speak at the funeral. I tried to avoid it, but it was no use. Funerals are a bit of a showcase in Jamaica, and all my grandmother's living children and grandchildren were to be on full display. My mother, once the prodigal daughter among her siblings, was now being praised because all of her children had gone to America and done well. So I bought a plane ticket and came home.

Sitting in the church at her funeral, I stared at the ornate stained-glass windows where beams of orange and green light filtered in. How familiar the choir sounded as they mournfully dragged out each syllable of the hymns. Vividly, I could see myself sitting next to my grandmother on Sunday mornings, holding her Bible because I was quickest at finding the passages that she loved.

When it was my turn to speak, I walked up to the pulpit ready to share with the congregation my abiding love for my grandmother. As I looked out at all the mourners, I realized the church was overflowing. Never had I witnessed so many people crowded into the pews. A typical Sunday morning saw only a handful of congregants; with the exception of Easter the church was seldom more than half filled. But on this day, people were standing next to the windows and spilling out of the open doors. It seemed that the entire village of Retreat was there, all four hundred and thirty-three residents, and they seemed as heartbroken at the loss of our matriarch as I was.

After I spoke, I went back to sit next to my mother. Amid the sadness, I couldn't help thinking how ridiculous it was that our family was so large. I leaned over to my mother and whispered: "It's just crazy that we have so many relatives. Did none of these people ever hear about birth control?"

"You know they are not birth family, don't you?" my mom responded.

I hadn't known. "But we brought food to them all the time," I said with surprise. "Grandma told us we were related."

My mother chuckled. She explained that my grandmother and her mother before her had been providing food to people in the village for as long as she could remember. As a child, she too had had to deliver evening meals. Now that I knew the truth, I was deeply touched by my family's legacy. Though we had little ourselves, we had more than those around us, so generations of my family had made sure that others didn't go hungry.

Today, as the president of the GrassROOTS Community Foundation, this is one of my main goals—to gather resources and share them with others in need. As one of our many charitable efforts, for the past eight years we have hosted an annual Turkey Drive. To date, we have provided almost eight thousand meals to the elderly and families in need during the holidays. With so much food on the planet, it is unconscionable that so many vulnerable adults and children do not have enough to eat, but my grandmother's example showed me that we can do something about that, starting on the smallest scale.

My daughter has been at my side throughout, along with her father and many other volunteers. We distribute food in some neighborhoods that are considered dangerous and have high levels of crime and poverty. The people there are no different from those in your neighborhood or mine; they have aspirations and dreams and their own personal stories. We all deserve to be treated with dignity.

Beyond teaching Marley about food insecurity, I am passing on a lesson that my grandmother handed down to me: To whom much is given, much is expected. You must lift as you climb by sharing what you have with others. And I don't only mean food.

In one way, the rationale for giving is purely selfish: When your community does well, so will you. A rising tide lifts all boats, right? Of course, when the community suffers, so will you. That suffering may at first be hard to see, but eventually it becomes clear. For example, if others around you are underinformed while you are educated, then they are likely to elect tyrants to office. If others around you are hungry while you have abundance, they may break into your home for food. As Martin Luther King Jr. stated in his famous "Letter from a Birmingham Jail": "I am cognizant of the interrelatedness of all communities and states . . . We are caught in an inescapable network of mutuality, tied in a single garment of destiny. Whatever affects one directly, affects all indirectly. Never again can we afford to live with the narrow, provincial 'outside agitator' idea."

I admit that, having been trained as a sociologist, I am at an advantage here. Yet, my fundamental understanding of the interconnectedness of all states of consciousness and being did not result from my formal training. It was instilled in me by my grandmother who had only a sixth-grade education. She understood that large external forces shape people's lives, that some people are born into families with limited resources while others are born into families with unlimited resources, and that many of us fall somewhere in between. Though she was not formally educated, she read the newspaper and her Bible daily. She voted, talked to her neighbors, and participated in the life of her church. She was aware that sometimes able-bodied people cannot find work because there is not enough work to go around, and that sometimes sick people cannot afford medical care. She knew that she had more resources than others because she had some land; therefore, being better positioned than most, she should share her good fortune.

My grandmother also taught us to be skeptical of any political efforts that did not put the needs of the people first. But she went even further, arguing that to sow good in the world you don't have to actually know or feel kinship with the people you are helping, but you do have to see the value in helping them. Choosing to stand up for others, even when you feel they would not support you in return, demands a commitment to something greater than your own wounded ego or even the immediate needs of the other person. It requires a dedication to fostering love and equity in the world. It asks us to see beyond this moment to the hope and promise that the person we are helping will one day reciprocate by helping someone else when given the chance.

We must coach our girls to become more than bystanders in this world. The research of sociologist Dr. Tamara Leech of Montclair State University and social worker Dr. Raphael Travis on positive youth development shows that when youth are able to actively engage in their community, they begin to develop a sense of themselves as leaders. Such engagement facilitates what we scholars refer to as the all-important five Cs: competence, confidence, connection, character, and caring. But social science research aside, as individuals in society, young or old, each of us is obliged to do our part, and we certainly don't need advanced degrees to do it. All we need is a mind that understands that others have needs, a heart that cares enough to do something about it, and a willingness to use our own resources to help.

15

Ignite Social Action

~~~~~~

Becoming more informed, with understanding and care, puts us in a good position to engage in social action. But as a reminder, the goal of the book is not for you to develop a girl whose job will be a *social activist*. Being a change-maker is not a job; we are not raising our children to have this as their occupational title. We are fostering joy and change-making within our girls. Your girl can be a change-making photographer, businesswoman, teacher, engineer, or dancer. She can use her passions to make the world a better place no matter where she lives and what position she holds. Our society is riddled with inequities, and the work of making it a more equitable place demands that we all use our various skills and talents.

But if you are like me, you want to know if what you are putting in is actually taking hold. Is your child really learning anything? Does she understand that she can indeed make a difference now and in the future? Is all this effort . . . *worth it*?

There is not a quick answer. Sometimes an event or a situation will arise where evidence of your labor reveals itself clearly. Other times you can feel like you are on a hunt, trying to figure out exactly whether your hard labor really matters.

At GrassROOTS, we, too, are interested in the progress of our girls' learning; luckily we have the luxury of observing girls' growth over time, since, typically, girls participate in our program for four to five years.

At the end of the fourth year of SuperCamp, I made the decision that we needed to evaluate the extent to which our girls were understanding and internalizing the core messages of our leadership-training program. Our board concurred, and after some discussion, we agreed that by the time our girls reached middle school (sixth grade), they would be asked to complete a social action project. We agreed that though we could help each girl, she would need to direct the project herself—so that each girl could explore her own interests. Further, this approach would allow us to evaluate a girl's ability to initiate, plan, execute, and complete a project. The expectations were that some girls would be more successful than others, and we would use the experience of developing the project to learn with them, bolster their training, reevaluate the curriculum, and refine our work.

You may be wondering, what *is* a social action project? Social action projects are inquiry-based learning campaigns that assess leadership development skills through a social justice framework. (See pages 194–96 for a list of some SuperGirls' social action projects.) Adults and caregivers provide time and support to facilitate the initiative, but each girl determines her areas of interest and poses her original questions that she wants to better understand.

Each social action project starts by identifying a key social issue of interest. Rather than telling girls what they need to see as a problem, girls are encouraged to share their stories of social frustrations—things they see happening that they wish they could change. This ideation stage consists of adults asking questions to better understand the source of the frustration. The girls' responses help us gauge whether they understand the distinction between personal troubles (something that is limited to a few individuals due to their own actions) or social issues (something that affects a lot of people and is connected to how society is structured).

A starting point of our early conversations comes from responses to these questions: *What are some of the things in the world you wish you could change? What are you going to do about them?*

It is important that girls understand that they—not their caregivers—are the solution-makers. This means that they must do an inventory of their own personal resources, which includes their skills, talents, and passions.

With my help and that of their family and friends, girls host listening sessions and small-group discussions with their peers to identify strategies about the best approach to their projects. This iterative process takes several weeks but is well worth it due to several key benefits. It enhances girls' learning experiences, fosters their curiosity, deepens their understanding of the issues they are interested in, and allows them to own their learning.

In terms of issues of social justice, a social action project gives girls a chance to understand the relationship between individual problems and social issues. It moves them from a sense of entitlement toward a sense of responsibility and teaches them the importance of advocacy, sharing, and responsibility.

The entire process is one of discovery. The girl must consistently problem solve, and caregivers consistently learn more about their girl's level of confidence, skills, passions, and understanding of social issues. And if all goes well, a girl should learn to:

- initiate ideas,
- galvanize peers,
- garner community support, and
- execute a project.

Here are some examples of what our SuperGirls have done over the past five years. I hope it will serve as a guide for your girl:

- **#1000BlackGirlBooks:** initiative aimed at collecting and donating one thousand books in which Black girls are the main characters. Ten-year-old Marley Dias's favorite activity was reading. In her fifth grade class, she noticed that none of the books assigned at school featured anyone who looked like her. She responded by launching a book drive called #1000BlackGirlBooks with the goal of collecting one thousand books featuring Black girls and Black women protagonists. She exceeded her goal and now has collected over twelve thousand books, donating most of them to communities across the globe. In February 2016, she donated her first 1,700 books to Retreat Primary School in St. Mary, Jamaica, and continues to donate books around the world. She has also created an online public resource guide with titles of the first thousand books.

- **#MathWizGames:** STEM-based games aimed at improving girls' confidence in mathematics. Eleven-year-old Amina loved math but was beginning to lose her confidence. She felt like she was being pushed out of the discipline and other girls were being pushed out too. In August 2016, she organized the MathWizGames, a day of fun, math-inspired games for girls in grades 1 to 6 with the goal of helping them build their math confidence.

- **#RoomForChange:** a room renovation project for unaccompanied minors living at the Newark YMCA. Twelve-year-old Brianna loved animals, science, and crafts and enjoyed making things. For her social action project, she adopted six bedrooms on the sixth floor of the Newark YMCA, which temporarily houses unaccompanied minors. The Essex County Court usually places these children at the YMCA because their parents or guardians are unable to care for them. Brianna's mission was to create warm spaces where children can feel safe and comfortable during their stay.

- **#FullCourtDress:** charity basketball game to collect winter coats for youth in Newark. Twelve-year-old Tori bridged her love of basketball and her commitment to helping homeless Newark youth and their families by hosting #FullCourtDress, a youth-led charity basketball game. Held in October, #FullCourtDress collected over one hundred winter coats, hats, scarves, gloves, and warm socks to benefit families at the Newark YMCA and Covenant House–Newark.

- **#Food4Life Summit:** a program aimed at educating youth and adults about healthy eating. Thirteen-year-old Huntar has a rare blood disorder that affects her blood count. Eating healthy is part of her medicine. Huntar, passionate about making sure that people eat healthy, chose to create a fun-filled afternoon of games and food demonstrations to teach kids and families about eating well and staying healthy.

- **#ZenZone:** a wellness go-box for youth coping with chronic pain. Diagnosed with juvenile idiopathic arthritis at age five, Ariyan has maintained a jovial spirit despite her invisible pain. For her social action project, ten-year-old Ariyan raised awareness of chronic illness. She created the ZenZone: a go-box to provide comfort to youth coping with chronic pain. On Sunday, June 2, 2019, at the Arthritis Foundation's Walk to a Cure in South Mountain Reservation, West Orange, New Jersey, Ariyan distributed fifty of her one hundred zen boxes. This event was the largest gathering of the arthritis community in the world, raising funds for resources and research to find better treatments and a cure.

- **#WhatOrphansWant:** a benefit concert to raise funds to grant wishes to orphaned youth. Thirteen-year-old Olivia Raymond loves to sing. In June 2019, she launched #WOW: What Orphans Want—a benefit concert that raised funds to grant wishes to orphan youth. She raised twelve thousand dollars; she used some of these funds to travel to Haiti, where she donated five thousand dollars to Child Hope International and used the rest of the funds to purchase gifts—including a cow, goats, and bicycles for 150 youth.

ASSIGNMENTS

Identify the resources you have to share.

Take out that paper and pen again and write this down: What do I have in abundance? Time? Money? Access to people? Transportation? Are these resources that I can share with others? (It is important that you give in ways that do not cause you undue constraints.) Then, start a second column next to each item and think of how you can use each resource for others productively.

Mentor a young person.

Invite her (or him) into your home. Work with her over time to help her identify, work toward, and attain her aspirations. Show your girl that giving of yourself—sharing your resources—is an intimate act.

Develop a community service or social action project.

Parents and girls can develop their own individual social action project, but most likely as the caregiver you will be seeking to support your girl. To that end, find or create a project that allows you or your girl the opportunity not only to share physical resources but also to transfer some of your skills and capital. If you are a middle-class person, choose to extend some of your creative, emotional, and intellectual capital to help change someone's circumstances. You and your girl are in the position to engender life-altering transformations in others. This is joyful, satisfying work.

The process of supporting and collaborating with your girl on her social action project will help you better understand why you must parent like it matters. It will reveal to you a simple truth: We are the ones we have been waiting for.

We are the solution-makers we want to see. We can find answers to some of the most intractable problems in the world, and the way forward lies within our parenting practice. We can create a new world through the way we parent, specifically through the way we invest in our girls. By arming our girls with knowledge of self and the world, by teaching them reason and demonstrating for them that passions and talents can be used to address social issues, and by ensuring that they see value in connections, we are laying the foundation for a better world.

Though our lives will be over one day, by raising joyful, change-making girls, we are making a choice to leave the world better than we found it. While no single action we take will determine who our girls become, our actions in totality will shape how they see the world and whether they, too, are willing to help create a better world. If we want social change and greater equity, we must begin with the children in our lives.

We can extend our greatest influence and leave a legacy of justice through the way we parent. Children are our best chances of creating a just world. To that end, we must cultivate in our girls the habit of giving their best effort at every turn. We must protect, love, and nurture these future change-makers as they grow; open up previously unimagined worlds to them; foster their resiliency; and encourage empathy, optimism, and joy within them.

Doing their best ensures not only their pursuit of excellence, but also their resolve to never quit on themselves and their dreams that a better world is possible.

How to Conduct a Social Action Project

Name your frustrations.
- What do you see in your neighborhood, community, or school that you wish you could change?
- What are *you* going to do about it?

Identify your passions.
What are your passions? What are some of the things you enjoy doing the most? Could or would you be happy to do it without being pushed?

Become informed.
- What do you know about the issue?
- Is the frustration personal or does it affect others?
- How many people are affected?

Develop a goal.
- What is your goal?
- What would it look like if you reached your goal?
- Who would be happy?
- If you were successful, what would change in your community?

Marshal your resources and make a plan.
- What resources do you need to help make the project happen?
- In addition to money, what type of people do you need?
- What talents do they need to best help you?

Acknowledgments

I cannot believe I am writing acknowledgments to my book. Totally surreal! There is no way that I could have gotten here without a full village of folks.

I will be overusing the words *grateful* and *thankful* because they best capture my emotions.

I feel forever grateful to Marley D. and Scotty for encouraging me to do this. Though she thought I could do it, I wasn't sure. And in truth, if it were not for Jacqueline Woodson's encouragement and support, I would not have done it. I remain in awe of her talent—she writes books for real. But as talented as she is, the best part of her for me is her heart. She is one of the most generous and loving people I have ever met. Her family, each of them—Juliet, Jackson, and Toshi—have embraced us so much and their kindness has been a source of inspiration. I also love her irrational belief in me. I am equally grateful for her patience. She has taken all my anxious phone calls and kept me inspired.

It was also Jacqueline who introduced me to Charlotte Sheedy, whom no one can deny. Her tenacious spirit can drive anyone to become better than we are. This book is made possible because they were convinced I had something to say. And if they believed it, who was I to be so uncertain?

But as with most things, this book, like my life, is a testimony to mothers. It was an orchestra of mothers that helped me get through this experience. Rosemarie Robotham, whom I affectionately call the GIFT, and Leslie Weaver reminded me that there are more and different words in me even when I feel empty. I wish I could think and write like them. Maybe on book two I will come close.

I feel completely grateful to Lisa Maxwell and Sonia Fergus, because their vision of me made me work hard each day. I felt like I had to live up to their expectations of me. For a decade they have insisted that I make my thoughts and ideas more known to the world and for ten years I have balked at them. I know they finally feel vindicated, because their cajoling worked and now there is a book.

I feel honored to have a set of moms whose parenting practices teach me so much about the value and importance of loving ourselves like we love our children. They are Aja, Mary, Carol, and Rakia, and they are my mommy north stars.

And then there is Andra Miller, my editor. I am convinced that Obatala guided her to me. She engendered such confidence in me when I had none. There were so many times that I wanted to give up, but I appreciate that she kept encouraging me to keep going.

These mothers, who parent like it matters, are my anchors.

I also have great friends who have helped me through this process. There are too many to name them all here, but I want them to know that I am grateful for their loving support.

I do want to mention a few: Sherille, Griselda, Nikki, Page, Tracy, and Tia, thank you for always asking me every moment about the book. I hope you like it. I thought of you as I wrote.

As you can imagine, no one writes a book in full isolation. There were countless nights when I just needed a second or third set of eyes. I am so grateful for PC, aka Margaret Collins, and Sabrina Curtis for taking the time to read and comment; I am forever grateful.

None of this would be possible without the SuperFamilies and the SuperGirls, who continue to teach me so much about myself, the value of parenting, and the need for all of us to invest in girls. They have given me a priceless gift and I am forever grateful.

I also owe a special thank-you to the original GrassROOTS team of Dr. Sandra Lewis, Michelle Alcaraz, Ohenewaa White, Susan James, Sheila Flemming-Hunter, Patrice Barnett, and Sabrina Webb, who helped me along the way. Because of you, I am.

A huge thank-you to the team at Ballantine, especially Elana Seplow-Jolley, who worked so hard to make sure that I offer an accessible, kind, and thoughtful book. I have found a home here with you. Thank you for making me feel seen and valued.

I have lived in nine U.S. states, and with each move I have learned more about myself. I am grateful to the people of Retreat, St. Mary, Kintyre, Jamaica; Philadelphia, Pennsylvania; Ann Arbor, Michigan; and Newark and West Orange, New Jersey, for helping me become what I am becoming. To the institutions that trained me to study, imagine, and lead—Boston Latin Academy, Brandeis, Temple, and the University of Michigan—thank you.

This has been the experience of a lifetime and I am overwhelmed with emotion.

Finally, to thank my mother, who inherited a legacy of pain and resilience, know that I appreciate all that you have poured into me. You created a framework for me to thrive. You are my safety net. There is no love without safety. I know and value you more than words can describe.

Appendix A

Living the Guiding Philosophies

GrassROOTS Community Foundation aims to create a world where *all* girls grow up to be healthy women.

Maat, an ancient Egyptian philosophy and strategy, guides our programming, as well as our interactions with families.

Based on Maat, we use a refined formula for achieving harmony in ourselves, our families, and our communities.

Truth + Order + Balance + Reciprocity = Harmony

Maat offers a powerful foundation for all of us to thrive so that we may live our lives in four-part harmony.

Below is a brief overview of these guiding principles.

TRUTH means that we honor the good, talents, and abilities that all human beings bring to the world. We also make it a practice to speak truth and do the right thing even when no one is watching.

Here are a few examples of truth in action:

- We respectfully acknowledge community members' gifts and talents.
- We celebrate ourselves and others.
- We express gratitude and say thank you to those who support us.

ORDER reminds us to be strategic—that there are methods and approaches to problem-solving and timing activities. We create routines as well as exercise flexibility in planning and implementing goals, so we know the sequence in which to execute things. Each girl sets a goal and develops an affirmation to support her growth toward it.

Here are a few examples of order in action:

- We honor and assist our elders because they came before us.
- We wait and listen to others speak and pay attention while they are sharing information.

BALANCE fosters our ability to use our resources wisely. Resources include our family, friends, and time. Balance helps us make the most of our resources in any given moment.

Here are a few examples of balance in action:

- We critique each other in kind, respectful, and compassionate ways.
- We organize our activities, including our time, to complete our task. We make time to transition as well as time to rest so that we do not overextend and exhaust ourselves.
- We ask for help when needed.

RECIPROCITY is both the practice of sharing good with others and being grateful for the good that surrounds us.

Here are some examples of reciprocity in action:

- If we see gaps in information and resources, we offer to help.
- We engage in activities that build our communities and improve members' access to resources.
- We collaborate.

HARMONY is the result of practicing these four core principles of Maat: Truth, Order, Balance, and Reciprocity. This practice cultivates flow and a sense of rhythm among the various aspects of our programming and work together. Harmony supports our efforts to work through challenges and develop strategies that keep us inspired and moving toward our goal of creating a world where all girls grow up to be healthy women.

Appendix B

SuperCamp Assessment

Name: Amina
Affirmation: I am compassionate.
Parents/Caregivers: Lisa Maxwell and family

Child's goals
1. Be more compassionate when it comes to calling my family and showing support when I hear sad things.
2. Be present.

Parents' goals for Amina
1. Daily journaling about inner feelings/thoughts/ideas
2. Develop better sequencing for tasks/projects and follow through
3. Assert point of view verbally in face of conflict
4. Compassionate giving

Child's self-observations
1. Gifts & Talents: Singing, Swimming, Dancing, Acting
2. Amina indicates that the most difficult thing to do is not getting irritated at friends when they get into an argument. She states the worst thing about being a girl is being emotional.
3. Amina expresses a desire to grow up to pursue her dreams and make a change in the world.
4. Amina acknowledges that she is happy most of the time but feels sad some of the time. She likes loving people who "love me even through all my differences."

Child's observed challenges according to caregivers

1. Starts tasks last minute and does not complete them
2. Avoids conflict
3. Does not see the connection between others' challenging circumstances and her station in life

Child's observed challenges

1. Amina has difficulty staying still and lying with her eyes closed in quiet.
2. Amina seems to choose to do the wrong thing even when she knows what's right.
3. Amina seems to get caught up in a moment of enjoyment and having fun and loses focus on greater goals or standards of behavior.

SuperCamp Research

1. Person: Queen Amina of Zaria
2. Place: Sudan
3. Poem: "We Wear the Mask" by Paul Laurence Dunbar

Recommendations/Action Steps
Truth
Recommendation
Increase her exposure to sacred texts and spiritual teachings about the nature and role of human beings on earth.

Action Steps
Purchase and read sacred stories written for children. Discuss them as a family. Consider *Sixteen Mythological Stories of Ifa* by Chief FAMA.

Recommendations
1. Explore her understanding of who she is in the world and her role as a member of the human family.
2. Develop a list of Amina's positive character traits, including

traits like compassion that parents would like her to develop.

Action Steps

1. Make a family activity of creating artwork, dance performances, and dramatic presentations that reflect core character traits that Amina has and that she needs to develop.
2. Post the artwork in her room or in prominent places. Make it the wallpaper for her home screen on her phone, computer, iPad, etc.
3. Each morning, the first thing she needs to do is focus on her character and who she came to the world to be. Simply focusing on the picture or focusing on a character trait as she brushes her teeth can accomplish this.
4. Put each character trait in a basket and let her choose one to focus on each day.
5. Talk about the relevance of the chosen character traits as they relate to personal, family, and community growth.
6. Have Amina create a SuperStar Shero based on the chosen character traits. She must create a name that reflects how the traits help others and her community. Have her write a story that indicates how a SuperStar Shero with her characteristics would help the world.

Recommendation

Increase her exposure to role models who demonstrate commitment to their truth and doing good in the world.

Action Steps

Have Amina research a different woman of African descent each month and report on her. Her report can be a dramatization, a PowerPoint, a collage. Make it fun and engaging. However, she is to focus on their character traits and how they changed the world around them. In addition, have her examine how the women overcame challenges.

Recommendation

Identify people/loved ones who are willing to engage Amina in discussions and activities that support understanding and embodiment of her truth.

Action Steps

Ask your team of caregivers and supporters to assist with these activities.

Order

Recommendation

Develop a weekly schedule of activities and responsibilities.

Action Steps

1. Create a to-do list that includes detailed steps and times for activities. The to-do list can become her business endeavor. Completing a task is taking care of her business. She can give her business a name like World Change Organization or I Do Good, LLC. Have her choose a name that resonates for her.

2. Have her connect the items on her list to her character traits and how these things help her grow into the person she came to the world to be. You can choose one a week. Eventually, she should develop the skill of connecting what she does to who she is in truth.

Recommendation

Engage in activities that support and foster emotional development including identifying, understanding, and expressing emotions.

Action Steps

1. Explore her emotional world with kid-friendly strategies.

   a. Teach her how to recognize and name feelings. Teach her that feelings are "information." They are "signals." They help us think about how best to approach a situation and keep ourselves safe. They increase our awareness of the challenges we face.

b. Play games similar to charades that allow her to act out emotions. In this case she should identify the thoughts and bodily sensations associated with each emotion.

2. Have her choose a color she likes and talk about how the color makes her feel. What thoughts does it bring up? Do some colors leave her feeling too sad? Do other colors get her too excited?

Recommendation

Explore conflict resolution and assertiveness practices with Amina.

Action Steps

Identify books that help children with conflict resolution, problem-solving, and assertiveness.

Balance

Recommendations

Increase her exposure to meditation and mindfulness practices.

Action Steps

1. Set up regular morning meditation times. These can be five to ten minutes.
2. Purchase mindfulness activity books for children. Consider works for children by Thich Nhat Hanh.

Recommendations

1. Continue work on the development of coping skills.
2. Engage her use of emotional recognition.

Action Steps

Have her come up with situations that are emotionally difficult and talk about how she can use her feelings to support her responses in various situations. This will give her an opportunity to review and learn from her challenges.

Reciprocity
Recommendation
Continue her community-giving activities.

Action Steps
Set up participation in charitable activities where she gives of herself and receives from the people who are receiving what she offers. If she works at a soup kitchen, she can sit and eat with another child and talk with them to find at least two things they have in common. Alternatively, she can sit with an adult and learn about the things they liked to do when they were children.

Recommendation
Develop a gratitude practice.

Action Step
Research indicates that gratitude is associated with positive academic, social, and emotional outcomes for adolescents. Amina can keep a journal or write items on a board before going to bed. She can make collages. Make it a fun family activity.

Appendix C

Project Reciprocity

In 2015, GrassROOTS wanted to evaluate whether the girls were understanding the principle of reciprocity. In collaboration with our local food bank we developed this project.

Food security means access by all people at all times to enough food for an active, healthy life.

In 2013, 14.3 percent of American households, 17.5 million, were food insecure. Food-insecure households (those with low and very low food security) had difficulty at some time during the year providing enough food for all their members due to a lack of resources. These individuals and families use emergency food relief to help them. Emergency food relief systems provide free food to needy persons through soup kitchens and food pantries.

Since 2000, food bank output has consistently increased. Research has not shown whether hunger is decreasing or whether there is a change in how food security is provided. Food pantries and soup kitchens have become symbols of hunger and poverty in the United States. The data indicate that significant numbers of individuals and families—many of whom are employed—are seeking food assistance.

GrassROOTS Community Foundation SuperCamp is partnering with Life Christian Church Soup Kitchen to help our Essex County community members in need. You can join us in this service action by signing your elementary or middle school–aged daughter up to serve our community members. Interested families must commit to five Saturdays between December 2014 and August 2015. By signing up you are agreeing to:

- Drop off your daughter by 10 A.M. and stay until 2 P.M. or until cleanup is complete;
- Make a contribution to the food pantry;
- Help your daughter submit a report about the spirit of giving based on her conversation with at least one person at the soup kitchen.

Resources

Understanding obesity
Centers for Disease Control and Prevention, cdc.gov/obesity/index.html

Understanding your body mass index
cdc.gov/healthyweight/assessing/bmi/index.html

ACEs, or Adverse Childhood Experiences
Take the Adverse Childhood Experiences Survey and get a sense of your exposure. It's available through the Centers for Disease Control and Prevention in Spanish and in English. Visit: cdc.gov/violenceprevention/acestudy/about.html

More about Maat
Lewis, Sandra. *Life in 4-Part Harmony: Get Everything in Your Life to Work with Everything Else in Your Life.* Oshun Golden Harvest Publishing, 2018.

To find a support group or a therapist
Get a recommendation from a physician or friend. You can also use online and community support groups. Build in an exploratory phase so that you can find the person or group that best meets your needs.

Psychology Today offers a database by state where you can find a therapist who deals with childhood trauma. Go to: psychologytoday.com/us/therapists/trauma-and-ptsd

Therapy for Black Girls: therapyforblackgirls.com/

Recommended readings

Morris, Monique. *Pushout: The Criminalization of Black Girls in Schools.* The New Press, 2016.

Bonilla-Silva, Eduardo. *Racism Without Racists: Color-Blind Racism and the Persistence of Racial Inequality in America.* Fifth edition. Rowman & Littlefield, 2017.

Recommended TED Talks

Nadine Burke Harris: "How Childhood Trauma Affects Health Across a Lifetime." ted.com/talks/nadine_burke_harris_how_childhood_trauma_affects_health_across_a_lifetime/transcript?language=en.

Martha Londagin: "Adverse Childhood Experiences Can Be Connectors to Joy." youtube.com/watch?v=0yMmJoRxxUY.

Monique Morris: "Why Black Girls Are Targeted for Punishment at Schools—and How to Change That." ted.com/talks/monique_w_morris_why_black_girls_are_targeted_for_punishment_at_school_and_how_to_change_that?language=en.

Mellody Hobson: "Color Blind or Color Brave?" ted.com/talks/mellody_hobson_color_blind_or_color_brave?language=en.

Camara Jones: "Allegories on Race and Racism." youtube.com/watch?v=GNhcY6fTyBM.

Kimberlé Crenshaw: "The Urgency of Intersectionality." ted.com/talks/kimberle_crenshaw_the_urgency_of_intersectionality?language=en.

Resources on how to understand and identify misinformation

Georgetown University Library: "Evaluating Internet Sources." library.georgetown.edu/tutorials/research-guides/evaluating-internet-content.

University of California Berkeley Library: "Weeding Out BS (Bad Sources)." lib.berkeley.edu/level-up/resources/weeding-out-bs.

Luvvie Ajayi: "5 Things to Do to Avoid Passing on Fake News on Social Media." awesomelyluvvie.com/2014/06/5-things-fake-news-social-media.html.

Browder, Atlantis T. *My First Trip to Africa.* Institute of Karmic Guidance, 1991.

Bibliography

Algoe, S. B., P. C. Dwyer, A. Younge, and C. Oveis. "A New Perspective on the Social Functions of Emotions: Gratitude and the Witnessing Effect." *Journal of Personality and Social Psychology,* vol. 119, no. 1 (2020), pp 40–74.

Baumrind, Diana. "Effects of Authoritative Parental Control on Child Behavior." *Child Development,* vol. 37, no. 4 (1966), pp. 887–907.

Bonilla-Silva, E., and D. Dietrich. "The Sweet Enchantment of Color-Blind Racism in Obamerica." *The Annals of the American Academy of Political and Social Science,* vol. 634, no. 1 (2011), pp. 190–206.

Brummelman, Eddie, Sander Thomaes, Geertjan Overbeek, Bram Orobio de Castro, Marcel A. van den Hout, and Brad J. Bushman. "On Feeding Those Hungry for Praise: Person Praise Backfires in Children With Low Self-Esteem." *Journal of Experimental Psychology: General*, vol. 143, no. 1 (Feb. 2014), pp. 9–14.

Burke, Kevin, and Stuart Greene. "Participatory Action Research, Youth Voices, and Civic Engagement." *Language Arts,* vol. 92, no. 6 (2015), 387–400.

Cassell, J., and K. Ryokai. "Making Space for Voice: Technologies to Support Children's Fantasy and Storytelling." *Personal and Ubiquitous Computing,* vol. 5, no. 3 (2001), pp. 169–90.

Fromm, Erich. *The Art of Loving.* New York: Harper Perennial Modern Classics, 2019.

Greco, M., and P. Stenner. "Happiness and the Art of Life: Diagnosing the Psychopolitics of Wellbeing." *Health, Culture and Society,* vol. 5, no. 1 (2013), pp. 1–19.

Henry, F., and C. Tator. *The Colour of Democracy: Racism in Canadian Society.* Toronto: Nelson Education, 2010.

Kiang, Lisa, et al. "Ethnic Identity and the Daily Psychological Well-Being of Adolescents from Mexican and Chinese Backgrounds." *Child Development*, vol. 77, no. 5 (2006), pp. 1338–50.

Lange, Brittany, Laura Callinan, and Megan Smith. "Adverse Childhood Experiences and Their Relation to Parenting Stress and Parenting Practices." *Community Mental Health Journal*, vol. 55, no. 4 (2019), pp. 651–62.

Lessing, Doris. *The Golden Notebook: A Novel.* New York: Harper Perennial Modern Classics, 2008.

Marin, Kelly, Jennifer Bohanek, and Robyn Fivush. "Positive Effects of Talking About the Negative: Family Narratives of Negative Experiences and Preadolescents' Perceived Competence." *Journal of Research on Adolescence*, vol. 18, no. 3 (2008), pp. 573–93.

McDonel, Jennifer S. "Exploring Learning Connections Between Music and Mathematics in Early Childhood." *Bulletin of the Council for Research in Music Education*, no. 203 (2015), pp. 45–62.

Minnard, Corrinne V. "A Strong Building: Foundation of Protective Factors in Schools." *Children & Schools*, vol. 24, no. 4 (October 2002), pp. 233–46.

Morris, Monique. *Pushout: The Criminalization of Black Girls in Schools.* New York: The New Press, 2016.

Oryan, S., and J. Gastil. "Democratic Parenting: Paradoxical Messages in Democratic Parent Education Theories." *International Review of Education* vol. 59, no. 1 (2013), pp. 113–129.

Peterson, Candida C., James L. Peterson, and John Carroll. "Television Viewing and Imaginative Problem Solving During Preadolescence." *Journal of Genetic Psychology*, vol. 147, no. 1 (1986), pp. 61–67.

Raine, Melissa. "From Boys to Men: Formations of Masculinity in Late Medieval Europe (Review)." *Parergon*, vol. 21, no. 1 (2004), pp. 190–92.

Reese, E., A. Bird, and G. Tripp. "Children's Self-Esteem and Moral Self: Links to Parent-Child Conversations Regarding Emotion." *Social Development*, vol. 16, no. 4 (2007), pp. 460–78.

Shipman, Claire, Katty Kay, and JillEllyn Riley. "How Puberty Kills Girls' Confidence." *The Atlantic*, September 20, 2018.

Snyder, Lisa, and Mark Snyder. "Teaching Critical Thinking and Problem Solving Skills." *Delta Pi Epsilon Journal*, vol. 50, no. 2 (2008), pp. 90–99.

Spagnola, Mary H., and Barbara Fiese. "Family Routines and Rituals: A Context for Development in the Lives of Young Children." *Infants & Young Children*, vol. 20, no. 4 (2007), pp. 284–99.

Sue, Derald Wing, ed. *Microaggressions and Marginality: Manifestation, Dynamics, and Impact.* Hoboken, N.J.: John Wiley & Sons, 2010, pp. 3–22.

Travis, R., and T. Leech. "Empowerment-Based Positive Youth Development: A New Understanding of Healthy Development for African American Youth." *Journal of Research on Adolescence*, vol. 24, no. 1 (2014), 93–116.

Utsey, S. O., M. H. Chae, C. F. Brown, and D. Kelly. "Effect of Ethnic Group Membership on Ethnic Identity, Race-Related Stress, and Quality of Life." *Cultural Diversity and Ethnic Minority Psychology*, vol. 8, no. 4 (2002), pp. 366–77.

Vale, Ronald D. "The Value of Asking Questions." *Molecular Biology of the Cell*, vol. 24, no. 6 (2013), pp. 680–82.

Valkenburg, P. M., and T.H.A van der Voort. "Influence of TV on Daydreaming and Creative Imagination: A Review of Research." *Psychological Bulletin*, vol. 116, no. 2 (1994), pp. 316–39.

Vallerand, R. J. "From Motivation to Passion: In Search of the Motivational Processes Involved in a Meaningful Life." *Canadian Psychology*, vol. 53, no. 1 (2012), pp. 42–52.

Van Dijk, M., S. Branje, L. Keijsers, S. Hawk, W. Hale, and W. Meeus. "Self-Concept Clarity Across Adolescence: Longitudinal Associations with Open Communication with Parents and Internalizing Symptoms." *Journal of Youth and Adolescence*, vol. 43, no. 11 (2014), pp. 1861–76.

Wall, Glenda. "'Love Builds Brains': Representations of Attachment and Children's Brain Development in Parenting Education

Material." *Sociology of Health & Illness,* vol. 40, no. 3 (2018), pp. 395–409.

Wall, Glenda. "Mothers' Experiences with Intensive Parenting and Brain Development Discourse." *Women's Studies International Forum,* vol. 33, no. 3 (2010), pp. 253–63.

For more about the UK's Foresight Challenge study: assets .publishing.service.gov.uk/government/uploads/system/uploads/ attachment_data/file/292453/mental-capital-wellbeing-summary.pdf.

For more about Kobi Kambon from the University of Alabama at Birmingham and his work on pan-African identity, see Jamison, D. F., "Kobi K. K. Kambon (Joseph A. Baldwin): Portrait of an African-Centered Psychologist," *Journal of Black Studies,* vol. 47, no. 6 (2016), pp. 592–609.

Research on obesity by Drs. Thomas Wadden and Albert Stunkard of the University of Pennsylvania School of Medicine can be found at med.upenn.edu/weight/wadden.html.

Michael Lamb's research focuses on forensic interviewing and the factors affecting children's adjustment. He and his colleagues have shown how developmentally sensitive interviewing improves the amount and quality of information obtained from young victims, witnesses, and offenders in investigative settings:

Pipe, M. E., M. Lamb, Y. Orbach, and A. C. Cederborg. *Child Sexual Abuse: Disclosure, Delay, and Denial.* New York: Routledge, 2007.

Lamb, M., I. Hershkowitz, Y. Orbach, and P. Esplin. *Tell Me What Happened: Structured Investigative Interviews of Child Victims and Witnesses.* Hoboken, N.J.: John Wiley & Sons, 2008.

Malloy, L., D. La Rooy, M. Lamb, and C. Katz. *Children's Testimony: A Handbook of Psychological Research and Forensic Practice.* Hoboken, N.J.: John Wiley & Sons, 2011.

Spencer, J., and M. Lamb. *Children and Cross-Examination: Time to Change the Rules?* Portland: Hart Publishing, 2012.

Lamb's other research has documented the roles played by parent-child relationships and other experiences in shaping children's adjustment and well-being:

Lamb, M. *The Role of the Father in Child Development.* Hoboken, N.J.: John Wiley & Sons, 2010.

Lamb, M. "Mothers, Fathers, Families, and Circumstances: Factors Affecting Children's Adjustment." *Applied Developmental Science,* vol. 16, no. 2 (2012), pp. 98–111.

General treatments of developmental science can be found in:

Lamb, M., and A. Freund. *The Handbook of Life-Span Development: Social and Emotional Development.* Hoboken, N.J.: John Wiley & Sons, 2010.

Bornstein, M., and M. Lamb. *Developmental Science: An Advanced Textbook.* 7th Edition. New York: Psychology Press, 2015.

DR. JANICE JOHNSON DIAS is a tenured associate professor of sociology at John Jay College in New York City. She is co-founder and president of the public health and social action organization GrassROOTS Community Foundation and leads its SuperCamp for girls. She holds a PhD in sociology from Temple University. Her collaborative work on Black girls' mental, sexual, and physical health issues earned her special congressional recognition and grants from the Robert Wood Johnson and Annie E. Casey foundations. Her work on the effects of safety on girls' physical activity in low-income neighborhoods led her to serve as an advisor to the City of Newark, where she focused on violence as a public health issue. Born in Jamaica, Dr. Janice Johnson Dias moved to the United States at age twelve and now lives in New Jersey with her husband, Scott, daughter, Marley, and dog, Philly.